The Mad Lover by John Fletcher

John Fletcher was born in December, 1579 in Rye, Sussex. He was baptised on December 20th.

As can be imagined details of much of his life and career have not survived and, accordingly, only a very brief indication of his life and works can be given.

Young Fletcher appears at the very young age of eleven to have entered Corpus Christi College at Cambridge University in 1591. There are no records that he ever took a degree but there is some small evidence that he was being prepared for a career in the church.

However what is clear is that this was soon abandoned as he joined the stream of people who would leave University and decamp to the more bohemian life of commercial theatre in London.

The upbringing of the now teenage Fletcher and his seven siblings now passed to his paternal uncle, the poet and minor official Giles Fletcher. Giles, who had the patronage of the Earl of Essex may have been a liability rather than an advantage to the young Fletcher. With Essex involved in the failed rebellion against Elizabeth Giles was also tainted.

By 1606 John Fletcher appears to have equipped himself with the talents to become a playwright. Initially this appears to have been for the Children of the Queen's Revels, then performing at the Blackfriars Theatre.

Fletcher's early career was marked by one significant failure; The Faithful Shepherdess, his adaptation of Giovanni Battista Guarini's Il Pastor Fido, which was performed by the Blackfriars Children in 1608.

By 1609, however, he had found his stride. With his collaborator John Beaumont, he wrote Philaster, which became a hit for the King's Men and began a profitable association between Fletcher and that company. Philaster appears also to have begun a trend for tragicomedy.

By the middle of the 1610s, Fletcher's plays had achieved a popularity that rivalled Shakespeare's and cemented the pre-eminence of the King's Men in Jacobean London. After his frequent early collaborator John Beaumont's early death in 1616, Fletcher continued working, both singly and in collaboration, until his own death in 1625. By that time, he had produced, or had been credited with, close to fifty plays.

Index of Contents

DRAMATIS PERSONAE

Astorax, King of Paphos.
Memnon, the General and the Mad Lover.
Polydor, Brother to Memnon, beloved of Calis.
Eumenes   } two eminent Souldiers.
Polybius   }
Chilax, an old merry Souldier.
Syphax, a Souldier in love with the Princess.
Stremon, a Souldier that can sing.
Demagoras, Servant to the General.
Chirurgion.
Fool.
Page.
Courtiers.
Calis, Sister to the King, and Mistris to Memnon.
Cleanthe, Sister to Syphax.
Lucippe, one of the Princesses Women.
Priestess of Venus, an old wanton.
A Nun.
Cloe, a Camp Baggage.

THE SCENE: Paphos.

THE MAD LOVER

PROLOGUE

To please all's impossible, and to despair
Ruins our selves, and damps the Writers care:
Would we knew what to doe, or say, or when
To find the mindes here equal with the men:
But we must venture; now to Sea we goe,
Faire fortune with us, give us room, and blow;
Remember ye're all venturers; and in this Play

How many twelve-peaces ye have 'stow'd this day:
Remember for return of your delight,
We launch, and plough through storms of fear, and spight:
Give us your fore-winds fairly, fill our wings,
And steer us right, and as the Saylor sings,
Loaden with Wealth, on wanton seas, so we
Shall make our home-bound-voyage chearfully;
And you our noble Merchants, for your treasure
Share equally the fraught, we run for pleasure.

ACTUS PRIMUS

SCENA PRIMA

Flourish.

Enter **ASTORAX**, King of Paphos, his Sister **CALIS**, **TRAIN**, and **CLEANTHE**, **LUCIPPE** Gentlewomen, at one door; at the other **EUMENES** a Souldier.

EUMENES
Health to my Soveraign.

KING
Eumenes, welcome:
Welcome to Paphos, Souldier, to our love,
And that fair health ye wish us, through the Camp
May it disperse it self, and make all happy;
How does the General, the valiant Memnon,
And how his Wars, Eumenes?

EUMENES
The Gods have giv'n you (Royal Sir) a Souldier,
Better ne're sought a danger, more approv'd
In way of War, more master of his fortunes,
Expert in leading 'em; in doing valiant,
In following all his deeds to Victories,
And holding fortune certain there.

KING
O Souldier,
Thou speak'st a man indeed; a Generals General,
A soul conceiv'd a Souldier.

EUMENES
Ten set Battels
Against the strong usurper Diocles

(Whom long experience had begot a Leader,
Ambition rais'd too mighty) hath your Memnon
Won, and won gloriously, distrest and shook him
Even from the head of all his hopes to nothing:
In three, he beat the Thunder-bolt his Brother,
Forc'd him to wall himself up: there not safe,
Shook him with warlike Engins like an Earthquake,
Till like a Snail he left his shell and crawl'd
By night and hideous darkness to destruction:
Disarm'd for ever rising more: Twelve Castles,
Some thought impregnable; Towns twice as many;
Countries that like the wind knew no command
But savage wildness, hath this General
With loss of blood and youth, through Storms and Tempests
Call'd to your fair obedience.

KING
O my Souldier
That thou wert now within my arms; what drums

[Drums within.

Are those that beat Eumenes?

EUMENES
His, my Soveraign;
Himself i'th' head of conquest drawing home,
An old man now to offer up his glories,
And endless conquest at your shrine.

KING
Goe all,
And entertain him with all Ceremonie,
We'l keep him now a Courtier.

EUMENES
Sir, a strange one,
Pray God his language bear it; by my life, Sir
He knows no complement, nor curious casting
Of words into fit places e're he speak 'em,
He can say fight well fellow, and I'le thank thee:
He that must eat, must fight; bring up the rear there,
Or charge that wing of horse home.

[Flourish.

KING
Goe too, goe too.

How many twelve-peaces ye have 'stow'd this day:
Remember for return of your delight,
We launch, and plough through storms of fear, and spight:
Give us your fore-winds fairly, fill our wings,
And steer us right, and as the Saylor sings,
Loaden with Wealth, on wanton seas, so we
Shall make our home-bound-voyage chearfully;
And you our noble Merchants, for your treasure
Share equally the fraught, we run for pleasure.

Flourish.

Enter **ASTORAX**, King of Paphos, his Sister **CALIS**, **TRAIN**, and **CLEANTHE**, **LUCIPPE** Gentlewomen, at one door; at the other **EUMENES** a Souldier.

EUMENES
Health to my Soveraign.

KING
Eumenes, welcome:
Welcome to Paphos, Souldier, to our love,
And that fair health ye wish us, through the Camp
May it disperse it self, and make all happy;
How does the General, the valiant Memnon,
And how his Wars, Eumenes?

EUMENES
The Gods have giv'n you (Royal Sir) a Souldier,
Better ne're sought a danger, more approv'd
In way of War, more master of his fortunes,
Expert in leading 'em; in doing valiant,
In following all his deeds to Victories,
And holding fortune certain there.

KING
O Souldier,
Thou speak'st a man indeed; a Generals General,
A soul conceiv'd a Souldier.

EUMENES
Ten set Battels
Against the strong usurper Diocles

(Whom long experience had begot a Leader,
Ambition rais'd too mighty) hath your Memnon
Won, and won gloriously, distrest and shook him
Even from the head of all his hopes to nothing:
In three, he beat the Thunder-bolt his Brother,
Forc'd him to wall himself up: there not safe,
Shook him with warlike Engins like an Earthquake,
Till like a Snail he left his shell and crawl'd
By night and hideous darkness to destruction:
Disarm'd for ever rising more: Twelve Castles,
Some thought impregnable; Towns twice as many;
Countries that like the wind knew no command
But savage wildness, hath this General
With loss of blood and youth, through Storms and Tempests
Call'd to your fair obedience.

KING
O my Souldier
That thou wert now within my arms; what drums

[Drums within.

Are those that beat Eumenes?

EUMENES
His, my Soveraign;
Himself i'th' head of conquest drawing home,
An old man now to offer up his glories,
And endless conquest at your shrine.

KING
Goe all,
And entertain him with all Ceremonie,
We'l keep him now a Courtier.

EUMENES
Sir, a strange one,
Pray God his language bear it; by my life, Sir
He knows no complement, nor curious casting
Of words into fit places e're he speak 'em,
He can say fight well fellow, and I'le thank thee:
He that must eat, must fight; bring up the rear there,
Or charge that wing of horse home.

[Flourish.

KING
Goe too, goe too.

[Enter **MEMNON**, and a train of **COURTIERS**, and **SOULDIERS**, two **CAPTAINS**, **CHILAX**.

Valiant and wise are twins Sir: welcom, welcom,
Welcom my fortunate and famous General,
High in thy Princes favour, as in fame,
Welcom to Peace, and Paphos.

MEMNON
Thank your Grace,
And would to God my dull tongue had that sweetness
To thank you as I should; but pardon me,
My sword and I speak roughly Sir: your battels
I dare well say, I have fought well; for I bring ye
That lazie end you wish for Peace, so fully,
That no more name of war is: who now thinks
Sooner or safer these might have been ended,
Begin 'em if he dare again; I'le thank him.
Souldier and Souldiers Mate these twenty five years,
At length your General, (as one whose merit
Durst look upon no less,) I have waded through
Dangers would damp these soft souls, but to hear of.
The maidenheads of thousand lives hang here Sir,
Since which time Prince, I know no Court but Marshal,
No oylie language, but the shock of Arms,
No dalliance but with death; No lofty measures
But weary and sad marches, cold and hunger,
Larums at midnight Valours self would shake at,
Yet I ne're shrunk: Balls of consuming Wildfire,
That lickt men up like lightning, have I laught at,
And tost 'em back again like childrens trifles.
Upon the edges of my Enemies swords
I have marcht like whirle-winds, fury at this hand waiting,
Death at my right; Fortune my forlorn hope,
When I have grapled with destruction,
And tug'd with pale fac'd Ruine, Night and Mischief,
Frighted to see a new day break in bloud;
And every where I conquer'd; and for you Sir,
Mothers have wanted wombs to make me famous,
And blown ambition, dangers; Those that griev'd ye,
I have taken order for i'th' earth: those fools
That shall hereafter—

KING
No more wars my Souldier:

[**KING** takes **MEMNON** aside and talks with him.

We must now treat of peace Sir.

CLEANTHE
How he talks,
How gloriously.

CALIS
A goodly timber'd fellow,
Valiant no doubt.

CLEANTHE
If valour dwell in vaunting;
In what a phrase he speaks, as if his actions
Could be set off in nothing but a noise;
Sure h'as a drum in's mouth.

CALIS
I wonder wenches
How he would speak to us.

CLEANTHE
Nothing but Larum,
Tell us whose throat he cut, shew us his sword,
And bless it for sure biting.

LUCIPPE
And 't like your Grace,
I do not think he knows us what we are,
Or to what end; for I have heard his followers
Affirm he never saw a woman that exceeded
A Sutlers wife yet, or in execution
Old bedrid Beldames without teeth or tongues,
That would not flie his furie? how he looks.

CLEANTHE
This way devoutly.

CALIS
Sure his Lordship's viewing
Our Fortifications.

LUCIPPE
If he mount at me,
I may chance choak his Battery.

CALIS
Still his eye
Keeps quarter this way: Venus grant his valour

Be not in love.

CLEANTHE
If he be, presently
Expect a Herald and a Trumpet with ye
To bid ye render; we two Perdu's pay for't else.

KING
I'le leave ye to my sister, and these Ladies
To make your welcom fuller: my good souldier
We must now turn your sternness into Courtship;
When ye have done there, to your fair repose Sir:

[Flourish.

I know you need it Memnon; welcom Gentlemen.

[Exit **KING**.

LUCIPPE
Now he begins to march: Madam the Van's yours,
Keep your ground sure; 'tis for your spurrs.

MEMNON
O Venus.

[He kneels amaz'd and forgets to speak.

CALIS
How he stares on me.

CLEANTHE
Knight him Madam, knight him,
He will grow toth' ground else.

EUMENES
Speak Sir, 'tis the Princess.

FIRST CAPTAIN
Ye shame your self, speak to her.

CALIS
Rise and speak Sir.
Ye are welcome to the Court, to me, to all Sir.

LUCIPPE
Is he not deaf?

CALIS
The Gentleman's not well.

EUMENES
Fie noble General.

LUCIPPE
Give him fresh air, his colour goes, how do ye?
The Princess will be glad Sir.

MEMNON
Peace, and hear me.

CLEANTHE
Command a silence there.

MEMNON
I love thee Lady.

CALIS
I thank your Lordship heartily: proceed Sir.

LUCIPPE
Lord how it stuck in's stomach like a surfeit.

CLEANTHE
It breaks apace now from him, God be thanked,
What a fine spoken man he is.

LUCIPPE
A choice one, of singular variety in carriage.

CLEANTHE
Yes and I warrant you he knows his distance.

MEMNON
With all my heart I love thee.

CALIS
A hearty Gentleman,
And I were e'en an arrant beast, my Lord,
But I lov'd you again.

MEMNON
Good Lady kiss me.

CLEANTHE
I marry, Mars, there thou cam'st close up to her.

CALIS
Kiss you at first my Lord? 'tis no fair fashion,
Our lips are like Rose buds, blown with mens breaths,
They lose both sap and savour; there's my hand Sir.

EUMENES
Fie, fie, my Lord, this is too rude.

MEMNON
Unhand me,
Consume me if I hurt her; good sweet Lady
Let me but look upon thee.

CALIS
Doe.

MEMNON
Yet—

CALIS
Well Sir,
Take your full view.

LUCIPPE
Bless your eyes Sir.

CALIS
Mercy,
Is this the man they talkt of for a Souldier,
So absolute and Excellent: O the Gods,
If I were given to that vanitie
Of making sport with men for ignorance,
What a most precious subject had I purchas'd!
Speak for him Gentlemen: some one that knows,
What the man ails; and can speak sense.

CLEANTHE
Sure Madam,
This fellow has been a rare Hare finder.
See how his eyes are set.

CALIS
Some one goe with me,
I'le send him something for his head, poor Gentleman,
He's troubled with the staggers.

LUCIPPE

Keep him dark,
He will run March mad else, the fumes of Battels
Ascend into his brains.

CLEANTHE
Clap to his feet
An old Drum head, to draw the thunder downward.

CALIS
Look to him Gentlemen: farewel, Lord I am sorry
We cannot kiss at this time, but believe it
We'l find an hour for all: God keep my Children,
From being such sweet Souldiers; Softly wenches,
Lest we disturb his dream.

[Exeunt **CALIS** and **LADIES**.

EUMENES
Why this is Monstrous.

FIRST CAPTAIN
A strange forgetfulness, yet still he holds it.

SECOND CAPTAIN
Though he ne're saw a woman of great fashion
Before this day, yet methinks 'tis possible
He might imagine what they are, and what
Belongs unto 'em: meer report of others.

EUMENES
Pish, his head had other whimsies in't: my Lord,
Death I think y'are struck dumb; my good Lord General.

FIRST CAPTAIN
Sir.

MEMNON
That I do love ye Madam; and so love ye
An't like your grace.

SECOND CAPTAIN
He has been studying this speech.

EUMENES
Who do ye speak to Sir?

MEMNON
Why where's the Lady,

CALIS
Kiss you at first my Lord? 'tis no fair fashion,
Our lips are like Rose buds, blown with mens breaths,
They lose both sap and savour; there's my hand Sir.

EUMENES
Fie, fie, my Lord, this is too rude.

MEMNON
Unhand me,
Consume me if I hurt her; good sweet Lady
Let me but look upon thee.

CALIS
Doe.

MEMNON
Yet—

CALIS
Well Sir,
Take your full view.

LUCIPPE
Bless your eyes Sir.

CALIS
Mercy,
Is this the man they talkt of for a Souldier,
So absolute and Excellent: O the Gods,
If I were given to that vanitie
Of making sport with men for ignorance,
What a most precious subject had I purchas'd!
Speak for him Gentlemen: some one that knows,
What the man ails; and can speak sense.

CLEANTHE
Sure Madam,
This fellow has been a rare Hare finder.
See how his eyes are set.

CALIS
Some one goe with me,
I'le send him something for his head, poor Gentleman,
He's troubled with the staggers.

LUCIPPE

Keep him dark,
He will run March mad else, the fumes of Battels
Ascend into his brains.

CLEANTHE
Clap to his feet
An old Drum head, to draw the thunder downward.

CALIS
Look to him Gentlemen: farewel, Lord I am sorry
We cannot kiss at this time, but believe it
We'l find an hour for all: God keep my Children,
From being such sweet Souldiers; Softly wenches,
Lest we disturb his dream.

[Exeunt **CALIS** and **LADIES**.

EUMENES
Why this is Monstrous.

FIRST CAPTAIN
A strange forgetfulness, yet still he holds it.

SECOND CAPTAIN
Though he ne're saw a woman of great fashion
Before this day, yet methinks 'tis possible
He might imagine what they are, and what
Belongs unto 'em: meer report of others.

EUMENES
Pish, his head had other whimsies in't: my Lord,
Death I think y'are struck dumb; my good Lord General.

FIRST CAPTAIN
Sir.

MEMNON
That I do love ye Madam; and so love ye
An't like your grace.

SECOND CAPTAIN
He has been studying this speech.

EUMENES
Who do ye speak to Sir?

MEMNON
Why where's the Lady,

The woman, the fair woman?

FIRST CAPTAIN
Who?

MEMNON
The Princess,
Give me the Princess.

EUMENES
Give ye counsel rather
To use her like a Princess: Fy my Lord,
How have you born your self, how nakedly
Laid your soul open, and your ignorance
To be a sport to all. Report and honour
Drew her to doe you favours, and you bluntly,
Without considering what, or who she was,
Neither collecting reason, nor distinction.

MEMNON
Why, what did I my Masters?

EUMENES
All that shews
A man unhandsom, undigested dough.

MEMNON
Did not I kneel unto her?

EUMENES
Dumb and sensless,
As though ye had been cut out for your fathers tomb,
Or stuck a land-mark; when she spoke unto you,
Being the excellence of all our Island,
Ye star'd upon her, as ye had seen a monster.

MEMNON
Was I so foolish? I confess Eumenes,
I never saw before so brave an outside,
But did I kneel so long?

EUMENES
Till they laught at ye,
And when you spoke I am asham'd to tell ye
What 'twas my Lord; how far from order;
Bless me, is't possible the wild noise of war
And what she only teaches should possess ye?
Knowledge to treat with her, and full discretion

Being at flood still in ye: and in peace,
And manly conversation smooth and civil,
Where gracefulness and glory twyn together,
Thrust your self out an exile?
Do you know Sir, what state she carries?
What great obedience waits at her beck continually?

MEMNON
She ne're commanded
A hundred thousand men, as I have done,
Nor ne're won battel; Say I would have kist her.

EUMENES
There was a dainty offer too, a rare one.

MEMNON
Why, she is a woman, is she not?

EUMENES
She is so.

MEMNON
Why, very well; what was she made for then?
Is she not young, and handsom, bred to breed?
Do not men kiss fair women? if they doe,
If lips be not unlawfull ware; Why a Princess
Is got the same way that we get a begger
Or I am cozen'd; and the self-same way
She must be handled e're she get another,
That's rudeness is it not?

SECOND CAPTAIN
To her 'tis held so, & rudeness in that high degree—

MEMNON
'Tis reason,
But I will be more punctual; pray what thought she?

EUMENES
Her thoughts were merciful, but she laught at ye,
Pitying the poorness of your complement,
And so she left ye. Good Sir shape your self
To understand the place, and noble persons
You live with now.

FIRST CAPTAIN
Let not those great deserts
The King hath laid up of ye, and the people,

Be blasted with ill bearing.

EUMENES
The whole name of souldier then will suffer.

MEMNON
She's a sweet one,
And good sirs leave your exhortations,
They come untimely to me, I have brains
That beat above your reaches: She's a Princess,
That's all: I have killed a King, that's greater.
Come let's to dinner, if the Wine be good,
You shall perceive strange wisdom in my blood.

[Exeunt all but **CHILAX**.

CHILAX
Well, would thou wert i' the wars again
Old Memnon, there thou wouldst talk toth' purpose,
And the proudest of all these Court Camelions
Would be glad to find it sense too: plague of this
Dead peace, this Bastard breeding, lowzie, lazie idleness,
Now we must learn to pipe, and pick our livings
Out of old rotten ends: these twenty five years
I have serv'd my Country, lost my youth and bloud,
Expos'd my life to dangers more than dayes;
Yet let me tell my wants, I know their answers,
The King is bound to right me, they good people
Have but from hand to mouth. Look to your wives
Your young trim wives, your high-day wives, your marchpanes,
For if the souldiers find not recompence,
As yet there's none a hatching; I believe
You men of wares, the men of wars will nick ye,
For starve nor beg they must not; my small means
Are gone in fumo: here to raise a better
Unless it be with lying, or Dog flattering,
At which our Nation's excellent; observing Dog-days,
When this good Lady broyles and would be basted
By that good Lord, or such like moral learnings,
Is here impossible; Well; I will rub among 'em
If any thing for honestie be gotten,
Though't be but bread and cheese I can be satisfied:
If otherwise the wind blow, stiff as I am
Yet I shall learn to shuffle: There's an old Lass
That shall be nameless yet alive, my last hope,
Has often got me my pocket full of crowns.
If all fail—Jack-Dawes, are you alive still?
Then I see the coast clear, when fools and boyes can prosper.

[Enter **FOOL** and **PAGE**.

PAGE
Brave Lieutenant.

FOOL
Hail to the man of worship.

CHILAX
You are fine sirs,
Most passing fine at all points.

FOOL
As ye see Sir,
Home-bred and handsome, we cut not out our clothes Sir
At half sword as your Taylors doe, and pink 'em
With Pikes and Partizans, we live retir'd Sir
Gentlemen like, and jealous of our honours.

CHILAX
Very fine Fool, and fine Boy, Peace playes with you,
As the wind playes with Feathers, dances ye,
You grind with all gusts, gallants.

PAGE
We can bounce Sir,
When you Soldados bend i'th' hams, and frisk too.

FOOL
When twenty of your trip-coats turn their tippets,
And your cold sallets without salt or vineger
Be wambling in your stomachs; hemp and hobnails
Will bear no price now, hangings and old harness
Are like to over-run us.

PAGE
Whores and hot houses.

FOOL
Surgeons and Syringes ring out your sance-bells.

PAGE
Your Jubile, your Jubile.

FOOL
Prob Deum.
How our St. Georges will bestride the Dragons,

The red and ramping Dragons.

PAGE
Advanc't fool—

FOOL
But then the sting i'th' tail boy.

PAGE
Tanto Melior.
For so much the more danger, the more honour.

CHILAX
You're very pleasant with our occupation Gent.
Which very like amongst these fierie Serpents
May light upon a Blind-worm of your blood,
A Mother or a Sister.

FOOL
Mine's past saddle,
You should be sure of her else: but say Sir Huon,
Now the Drums dubbs, and the sticks turn'd bed-staves,
All the old Foxes hunted to their holes,
The Iron age return'd to Erebus,
And Honorificabilitudinitatibus
Thrust out o'th' Kingdom by the head and shoulders,
What trade do you mean to follow?

CHILAX
That's a question.

FOOL
Yes and a learned question if ye mark it,
Consider and say on.

CHILAX
Fooling as thou dost, that's the best trade I take it.

FOOL
Take it straight then
For fear your fellows be before ye, hark ye Lieutenant
Fooling's the thing, the thing worth all your fightings,
When all's done ye must fool Sir.

CHILAX
Well, I must then.

FOOL

But do you know what fooling is? true fooling,
The circumstances that belong unto it?
For every idle knave that showes his teeth,
Wants and would live, can juggle, tumble, fiddle,
Make a dog face, or can abuse his fellow,
Is not a fool at first dash; you shall find Sir
Strange turnings in this trade; to fool is nothing
As fooling has been, but to fool the fair way,
The new way, as the best men fool their friends,
For all men get by fooling, meerly fooling,
Desert does nothing, valiant, wise, vertuous,
Are things that walk by without bread or breeches.

CHILAX

I partly credit that.

FOOL

Fine wits, fine wits Sir,
There's the young Boy, he does well in his way too,
He could not live else in his Masters absence;
He tyes a Ladyes garters so, so prettily,
Say his hand slip, but say so.

CHILAX

Why let it slip then.

FOOL

'Tis ten to one the body shall come after,
And he that works deserves his wages.

CHILAX

That's true.

FOOL

He riddles finely to a waiting Gentlewoman,
Expounds dreams like a Prophet, dreams himself too,
And wishes all dreams true; they cry Amen,
And there's a Memorandum: he can sing too
Bawdy enough to please old Ladies: he lies rarely,
Pawns ye a sute of clothes at all points, fully,
Can pick a pocket if ye please, or casket;
Lisps when he lists to catch a Chambermaid,
And calls his Hostess mother, these are things now,
If a man mean to live: to fight and swagger,
Beaten about the Ears with bawling sheepskins,
Cut to the soul for Summer: here an arm lost,
And there a leg; his honourable head
Seal'd up in salves and cereclothes, like a packet,

And so sent over to an Hospital, stand there, charge there,
Swear there, whore there, dead there,
And all this sport for cheese, and chines of dog-flesh,
And mony when two wednesdayes meet together,
Where to be lowzie is a Gentleman,
And he that wears a clean shirt has his shrowd on.

CHILAX
I'le be your scholar, come if I like fooling.

FOOL
You cannot choose but like it, fight you one day
I'le fool another, when your Surgeon's paid,
And all your leaks stopt, see whose slops are heaviest,
I'le have a shilling for a can of wine,
When you shall have two Sergeants for a Counter.

BOY
Come learn of us Lieutenant, hang your Iron up,
We'l find you cooler wars.

CHILAX
Come let's together,
I'le see your tricks, and as I like 'em.—

[Exeunt.

[Enter **MEMNON, EUMENES,** and **CAPTAINS**.

MEMNON
Why was there not such women in the camp then
Prepar'd to make me know 'em?

EUMENES
'Twas no place Sir.

FIRST CAPTAIN
Why should they live in Tumults? they are creatures
Soft and of sober natures.

MEMNON
Cou'd not your wives,
Your Mothers, or your Sisters have been sent for
To exercise upon?

EUMENES
We thank your Lordship.

SECOND CAPTAIN
But do you mean?

MEMNON
I do mean.

SECOND CAPTAIN
What Sir?

MEMNON
To see her,
And see thee hang'd too an thou anger'st me,
And thousands of your throats cut, get ye from me,
Ye keep a prating of your points of manners,
And fill my head with lowzie circumstances,
Better have Ballads in't, your courtly worships,
How to put off my hat, you, how to turn me,
And you (forsooth) to blow my nose discreetly;
Let me alone, for I will love her, see her,
Talk to her, and mine own way.

EUMENES
She's the Princess.

MEMNON
Why let her be the Devil, I have spoke
When Thunder durst not check me, I must love,
I know she was a thing kept for me.

EUMENES
And I know Sir,
Though she were born yours, yet your strange behaviour
And want—

MEMNON
Thou liest.

EUMENES
I do not.

MEMNON
Ha!

EUMENES
I do not lye Sir,
I say you want fair language, nay 'tis certain
You cannot say good morrow.

MEMNON
Ye Dog-whelps,
The proudest of your prating tongues—

EUMENES
Doe, kill us,
Kill us for telling truth: for my part, General,
I would not live to see men make a may-game
Of him I have made a Master, kill us quickly,
Then ye may—

MEMNON
What?

EUMENES
Doe what you list, draw your sword childishly
Upon your Servants that are bound to tell ye;
I am weary of my life.

FIRST CAPTAIN
And I.

SECOND CAPTAIN
And all Sir.

EUMENES
Goe to the Princess, make her sport, cry to her
I am the glorious man of war.

MEMNON
Pray ye leave me,
I am sorry I was angry, I'le think better,
Pray no more words.

EUMENES
Good Sir.

MEMNON
Nay then.

SECOND CAPTAIN
We are gone Sir.

[Exeunt **EUMENES** and **CAPTAIN**.

[Enter Princess **CALIS**, **LUCIPPE**, **CLEANTHE**.

CALIS

How came he hither? see for Heavens sake wenches,
What face, and what postures he puts on,

[**MEMNON** walks aside, full of strange gestures.

I do not think he is perfect.

CLEANTHE
If your love
Have not betray'd his little wits, he's well enough,
As well as he will be.

CALIS
Mark how he muses.

LUCIPPE
H'as a Batalia now in's brains, he draws out, now
Have at ye Harpers.

CLEANTHE
See, see, there the fire fails.

LUCIPPE
Look what an Alphabet of faces he runs through.

CLEANTHE
O love, love, how amorously thou look'st
In an old rusty armour.

CLEANTHE
I'll away, for by my troth I fear him.

LUCIPPE
Fear the gods, Madam,
And never care what man can do, this fellow
With all his frights about him and his furies,
His Larums, and his Launces, Swords, and Targets,
Nay case him up in armour Cap-a-pe,
Yet durst I undertake within two hours,
If he durst charge, to give him such a shake,
Should shake his Valour off, and make his shanks to ake.

CLEANTHE
For shame no more.

CALIS
He muses still.

CLEANTHE
The Devil—
Why should this old dryed timber chopt with thunder—

CALIS
Old Wood burns quickest.

LUCIPPE
Out, you would say Madam,
Give me a green stick that may hold me heat,
And smoak me soundly too; He turns, and sees ye.

[**MEMNON** comes to her.

CLEANTHE
There's no avoiding now, have at ye.

MEMNON
Lady.
The more I look upon ye.

[Stays her.

CLEANTHE
The more you may, Sir.

CALIS
Let him alone.

MEMNON
I would desire your patience.
The more I say I look, the more—

[Stays her.

LUCIPPE
My Fortune,
'Tis very apt, Sir.

MEMNON
Women, let my Fortune
And me alone I wish ye, pray come this way,
And stand you still there Lady.

CALIS
Leave the words Sir, and leap into the meaning.

MEMNON

Then again:
I tell you I do love ye.

CALIS
Why?

MEMNON
No questions: pray no more questions.
I do love you, infinitely: why do you smile?
Am I ridiculous?

CALIS
I am monstrous fearful, no, I joy you love me.

MEMNON
Joy on then, and be proud on't, I do love you,
Stand still, do not trouble me you Women.
He loves you Lady at whose feet have kneel'd
Princes to beg their freedoms, he whose valour
Has overrun whole Kingdoms.

CALIS
That makes me doubt, Sir,
'Twill overrun me too.

MEMNON
He whose Sword.

CLEANTHE
Talk not so big, Sir, you will fright the Princess.

MEMNON
Ha.

LUCIPPE
No forsooth.

CALIS
I know ye have done wonders.

MEMNON
I have and will do more and greater, braver;
And for your beauty miracles, name that Kingdom
And take your choice.

CALIS
Sir I am not ambitious.

MEMNON
Ye shall be, 'tis the Child of Glory: she that I love
Whom my desires shall magnifie, time stories,
And all the Empires of the Earth.

CLEANTHE
I would fain ask him—

LUCIPPE
Prithee be quiet, he will beat us both else.

CLEANTHE
What will ye make me then, Sir?

MEMNON
I will make thee
Stand still and hold thy peace; I have a heart, Lady.

CALIS
Ye were a monster else.

MEMNON
A loving heart,
A truly loving heart.

CALIS
Alas, how came it?

MEMNON
I would you had it in your hand, sweet Lady,
To see the truth it bears you.

CALIS
Do you give it.

LUCIPPE
That was well thought upon.

CLEANTHE
'Twill put him to't Wench.

CALIS
And you shall see I dare accept it, Sir,
Tak't in my hand and view it: if I find it
A loving and a sweet heart, as you call it,
I am bound, I am.

MEMNON

No more, I'll send it to ye,
As I have honour in me, you shall have it.

CLEANTHE
Handsomly done, Sir, and perfum'd by all means,
The Weather's warm, Sir.

MEMNON
With all circumstance.

LUCIPPE
A Napkin wrought most curiously.

MEMNON
Divinely.

CLEANTHE
Put in a Goblet of pure Gold.

MEMNON
Yes in Jacinth
That she may see the Spirit through.

LUCIPPE
Ye have greas'd him
For chewing love again in haste.

CLEANTHE
If he should do it.

CALIS
If Heaven should fall we should have larks; he do it!

CLEANTHE
See how he thinks upon't.

CALIS
He will think these three years
Ere he prove such an Ass, I lik't his offer,
There was no other way to put him off else.

MEMNON
I will do it—
Lady expect my heart.

CALIS
I do, Sir.

MEMNON

Love it, for 'tis a heart that—and so I leave ye.

[Exit **MEMNON**.

CLEANTHE

Either he is stark mad,
Or else I thinks he means it.

CALIS

He must be stark mad
Or else he will never do it, 'tis vain Glory,
And want of judgment that provokes this in him;
Sleep and Society cures all: his heart?
No, no, good Gentleman there's more belongs to't,
Hearts are at higher prices, let's go in
And there examine him a little better.
Shut all the doors behind for fear he follow,
I hope I have lost a lover, and am glad on't.

[Exeunt.

ACTUS SECUNDUS

SCENA PRIMA

Enter **MEMNON** alone.

MEMNON

'Tis but to dye, Dogs do it, Ducks with dabling,
Birds sing away their Souls, & Babies sleep 'em,
Why do I talk of that is treble vantage?
For in the other World she is bound to have me;
Her Princely word is past: my great desert too
Will draw her to come after presently,
'Tis justice, and the gods must see it done too.
Besides, no Brother, Father, Kindred there
Can hinder us, all languages are alike too.
There love is everlasting, ever young,
Free from Diseases, ages, jealousies,
Bawds, Beldames, Painters, Purgers: dye? 'tis nothing,
Men drown themselves for joy to draw in Juleps
When they are hot with Wine: In dreams we do it.
And many a handsom Wench that loves the sport well,
Gives up her Soul so in her Lovers bosome;
But I must be incis'd first, cut and open'd,

My heart, and handsomely, ta'n from me; stay there,
Dead once, stay, let me think again, who do I know there?
For else to wander up and down unwaited on
And unregarded in my place and project,
Is for a Sowters Soul, not an old Souldiers.
My brave old Regiments—I there it goes,
That have been kill'd before me, right.—

[Enter **CHILAX**.

CHILAX
He's here, and I must trouble him.

MEMNON
Then those I have conquer'd
To make my train full.

CHILAX
Sir.

MEMNON
My Captains then—

CHILAX
Sir, I beseech ye.

MEMNON
For to meet her there
Being a Princess and a Kings sole Sister
With great accommodation must be cared for.

CHILAX
Weigh but the Souldiers poverty.

MEMNON
Mine own Troop first
For they shall die.

CHILAX
How, what's this?

MEMNON
Next—

CHILAX
Shall I speak louder, Sir?

MEMNON

A square Battalia—

CHILAX
You do not think of us.

MEMNON
Their Armours gilded—

CHILAX
Good noble Sir.

MEMNON
And round about such Engines
Shall make Hell shake.

CHILAX
Ye do not mock me.

MEMNON
For, Sir,
I will be strong, as brave—

CHILAX
Ye may consider,
You know we have serv'd you long enough.

MEMNON
No Souldier
That ever landed on the blest Elyzium
Did or shall march, as I will.

CHILAX
Would ye would march, Sir,
Up to the King and get us—

MEMNON
King nor Keiser
Shall equal me in that world.

CHILAX
What a Devil ails he?

MEMNON
Next, the rare beauties of those Towns I fir'd.

CHILAX
I speak of money, Sir.

MEMNON
Ten thousand Coaches—

CHILAX
O pounds, Sir, pounds I beseech your Lordship,
Let Coaches run out of your remembrance.

MEMNON
In which the wanton Cupids, and the Graces
Drawn with the Western winds kindling desires,
And then our Poets—

CHILAX
Then our pay.

MEMNON
For Chilax when the triumph comes; the Princess
Then, for I will have a Heaven made—

CHILAX
Bless your Lordship!
Stand still, Sir.

MEMNON
So I do, and in it—

CHILAX
Death Sir,
You talk you know not what.

MEMNON
Such rare devices:
Make me I say a Heaven.

CHILAX
I say so too, Sir.

MEMNON
For here shall run a Constellation.

CHILAX
And there a pissing Conduit.

MEMNON
Ha!

CHILAX
With wine, Sir.

MEMNON
A Sun there in his height, there such a Planet.

CHILAX
But where's our money, where runs that?

MEMNON
Ha?

CHILAX
Money,
Money an't like your Lordship.

MEMNON
Why all the carriage shall come behind, the stuff,
Rich hangings, treasure;
Or say we have none.

CHILAX
I may say so truly,
For hang me if I have a Groat: I have serv'd well
And like an honest man: I see no reason—

MEMNON
Thou must needs die good Chilax.

CHILAX
Very well, Sir.

MEMNON
I will have honest, valiant souls about me,
I cannot miss thee.

CHILAX
Dye?

MEMNON
Yes die, and Pelius,
Eumenes and Polybius: I shall think
Of more within these two hours.

CHILAX
Dye Sir?

MEMNON
I, Sir,
And ye shall dye.

CHILAX
When, I beseech your Lordship?

MEMNON
To morrow see ye do dye.

CHILAX
A short warning,
Troth, Sir, I am ill prepar'd.

MEMNON
I dye my self then,
Beside there's reason—

CHILAX
Oh!

MEMNON
I pray thee tell me,
For thou art a great Dreamer.

CHILAX
I can dream, Sir,
If I eat well and sleep well.

MEMNON
Was it never
By Dream or Apparition open'd to thee—

CHILAX
He's mad.

MEMNON
What the other world was, or Elyzium?
Didst never travel in thy sleep?

CHILAX
To Taverns,
When I was drunk o're night; or to a Wench,
There's an Elyzium for ye, a young Lady
Wrapt round about ye like a Snake: is that it?
Or if that strange Elyzium that you talk of
Be where the Devil is, I have dream't of him,
And that I have had him by the horns, and rid him,
He trots the Dagger out o'th' sheath.

MEMNON

Elyzium,
The blessed fields man.

CHILAX
I know no fields blessed, but those I have gain'd by.
I have dream't I have been in Heaven too.

MEMNON
There, handle that place; that's Elyzium.

CHILAX
Brave singing, and brave dancing,
And rare things.

MEMNON
All full of flowers.

CHILAX
And Pot-herbs.

MEMNON
Bowers for lovers,
And everlasting ages of delight.

CHILAX
I slept not so far.

MEMNON
Meet me on those banks
Some two days hence.

CHILAX
In Dream, Sir?

MEMNON
No in death, Sir.
And there I Muster all, and pay the Souldier.
Away, no more, no more.

CHILAX
God keep your Lordship:
This is fine dancing for us.

[Enter **SIPHAX**.

SIPHAX
Where's the General?

CHILAX

There's the old sign of Memnon, where the soul is
You may go look as I have.

SIPHAX

What's the matter?

CHILAX

Why question him and see; he talks of Devils,
Hells, Heavens, Princes, Powers, and Potentates,
You must to th' pot too.

SIPHAX

How?

CHILAX

Do you know Elyzium? a tale he talks the Wild-goose chase of.

SIPHAX

Elyzium? I have read of such a place.

CHILAX

Then get ye to him,
Ye are as fine company as can be fitted.

[Exit **CHILAX**.

Your Worships fairly met.

SIPHAX

Mercy upon us,
What ails this Gentleman?

MEMNON

Provision—

SIPHAX

How his head works!

MEMNON

Between two Ribbs,
If he cut short or mangle me; I'le take him
And twirle his neck about.

SIPHAX

Now Gods defend us.

MEMNON

In a pure Cup transparent, with a writing
To signifie—

SIPHAX
I never knew him thus:
Sure he's bewitch'd, or poyson'd.

MEMNON
Who's there?

SIPHAX
I Sir.

MEMNON
Come hither, Siphax.

SIPHAX
Yes, how does your Lordship?

MEMNON
Well, God a mercy Souldier, very well,
But prithee tell me—

SIPHAX
Any thing I can, Sir.

MEMNON
What durst thou do to gain the rarest Beauty
The World has?

SIPHAX
That the World has? 'tis worth doing.

MEMNON
Is it so; but what doing bears it?

SIPHAX
Why! any thing; all danger it appears to.

MEMNON
Name some of those things: do.

SIPHAX
I would undertake, Sir,
A Voyage round about the World.

MEMNON
Short, Siphax.

A Merchant does it to spice pots of Ale.

SIPHAX
I wou'd swim in Armour.

MEMNON
Short still; a poor Jade
Loaden will take a stream and stem it strongly
To leap a Mare.

SIPHAX
The plague, I durst.

MEMNON
Still shorter,
I'll cure it with an Onion.

SIPHAX
Surfeits.

MEMNON
Short still:
They are often Physicks for our healths, and help us.

SIPHAX
I wou'd stand a breach.

MEMNON
Thine honour bids thee, Souldier:
'Tis shame to find a second cause.

SIPHAX
I durst, Sir,
Fight with the fellest Monster.

MEMNON
That's the poorest,
Man was ordain'd their Master; durst ye dye, Sir?

SIPHAX
How? dye my Lord!

MEMNON
Dye Siphax; take thy Sword,
And come by that door to her; there's a price
To buy a lusty love at.

SIPHAX

I am content, Sir,
To prove no Purchaser.

MEMNON
Away thou World-worm,
Thou win a matchless Beauty?

SIPHAX
'Tis to lose't Sir,
For being dead, where's the reward I reach at?
The love I labour for?

MEMNON
There it begins Fool,
Thou art meerly cozen'd; for the loves we now know
Are but the heats of half an hour; and hated
Desires stir'd up by nature to encrease her;
Licking of one another to a lust;
Course and base appetites, earths meer inheritours
And Heirs of Idleness and blood; Pure Love,
That, that the soul affects, and cannot purchase
While she is loaden with our flesh, that Love, Sir,
Which is the price of honour, dwells not here,
Your Ladies eyes are lampless to that Vertue,
That beauty smiles not on a cheek washt over,
Nor scents the sweet of Ambers; below, Siphax
Below us, in the other World Elyzium,
Where's no more dying, no despairing, mourning,
Where all desires are full, desarts down loaden,
There Siphax, there, where loves are ever living.

SIPHAX
Why do we love in this World then?

MEMNON
To preserve it,
The maker lost his work else; but mark Siphax,
What issues that love bears.

SIPHAX
Why Children, Sir.
I never heard him talk thus; thus divinely
And sensible before.

MEMNON
It does so, Siphax,
Things like our selves, as sensual, vain, unvented
Bubbles, and breaths of air, got with an itching

As blisters are, and bred, as much corruption
Flows from their lives, sorrow conceives and shapes 'em,
And oftentimes the death of those we love most.
The breeders bring them to the World to curse 'em,
Crying they creep amongst us like young Cats.
Cares and continual Crosses keeping with 'em,
They make Time old to tend them, and experience
An ass, they alter so; they grow and goodly,
Ere we can turn our thoughts, like drops of water
They fall into the main, are known no more;
This is the love of this World; I must tell thee
For thou art understanding.

SIPHAX
What you please, Sir.

MEMNON
And as a faithful man:
Nay I dare trust thee,
I love the Princess.

SIPHAX
There 'tis, that has fired him,
I knew he had some inspiration.
But does she know it, Sir?

MEMNON
Yes marry does she,
I have given my heart unto her.

SIPHAX
If ye love her.

MEMNON
Nay, understand me, my heart taken from me,
Out of my Body, man, and so brought to her.
How lik'st thou that brave offer? there's the love
I told thee of; and after death, the living;
She must in justice come Boy, ha?

SIPHAX
Your heart, Sir?

MEMNON
I, so by all means, Siphax.

SIPHAX
He loves roast well

That eats the Spit.

MEMNON
And since thou art come thus fitly,
I'll do it presently and thou shalt carry it,
For thou canst tell a story and describe it.
And I conjure thee, Siphax, by thy gentry,
Next by the glorious Battels we have fought in,
By all the dangers, wounds, heats, colds, distresses,
Thy love next, and obedience, nay thy life.

SIPHAX
But one thing, first, Sir, if she pleas'd to grant it,
Could ye not love her here and live? consider.

MEMNON
Ha? Yes, I think I could.

SIPHAX
'Twould be far nearer,
Besides the sweets here would induce the last love
And link it in.

MEMNON
Thou sayest right, but our ranks here
And bloods are bars between us, she must stand off too
As I perceive she does.

SIPHAX
Desert and Duty
Makes even all, Sir.

MEMNON
Then the King, though I
Have merited as much as man can, must not let her,
So many Princes covetous of her beauty;
I wou'd with all my heart, but 'tis impossible.

SIPHAX
Why, say she marry after.

MEMNON
No, she dares not;
The gods dare not do ill; come.

SIPHAX
Do you mean it?

MEMNON
Lend me thy knife, and help me off.

SIPHAX
For heaven sake,
Be not so stupid mad, dear General.

MEMNON
Dispatch, I say.

SIPHAX
As ye love that ye look for,
Heaven and the blessed life.

MEMNON
Hell take thee, Coxcomb,
Why dost thou keep me from it? thy knife I say.

SIPHAX
Do but this one thing, on my knees I beg it,
Stay but two hours till I return again.
For I will to her, tell her all your merits,
Your most unvalu'd love, and last your danger;
If she relent, then live still, and live loving,
Happy, and high in favour: if she frown—

MEMNON
Shall I be sure to know it?

SIPHAX
As I live, Sir,
My quick return shall either bring ye fortune,
Or leave you to your own fate.

MEMNON
Two hours?

SIPHAX
Yes, Sir.

MEMNON
Let it be kept, away, I will expect it.

[Exit **MEMNON**

[Enter **CHILAX**, **FOOL** and **BOY**.

CHILAX

You dainty wits! two of ye to a Cater,
To cheat him of a dinner?

BOY
Ten at Court, Sir,
Are few enough, they are as wise as we are.

CHILAX
Hang ye, I'le eat at any time, and any where,
I never make that part of want, preach to me
What ye can do, and when ye list.

FOOL
Your patience,
'Tis a hard day at Court, a fish day.

CHILAX
So it seems, Sir,
The fins grow out of thy face.

FOOL
And to purchase
This day the company of one dear Custard,
Or a mess of Rice ap Thomas, needs a main wit;
Beef we can bear before us lined with Brewes
And tubs of Pork; vociferating Veals,
And Tongues that ne're told lye yet.

CHILAX
Line thy mouth with 'em.

FOOL
Thou hast need, and great need,
For these finny fish-dayes,
The Officers understandings are so flegmatick,
They cannot apprehend us.

CHILAX
That's great pity,
For you deserve it, and being apprehended
The whip to boot; Boy what do you so near me?
I dare not trust your touch Boy.

[Enter **STREMON** and his **BOY**.

BOY
As I am vertuous,
What, thieves amongst our selves?

CHILAX
Stremon.

STREMON
Lieutenant.

CHILAX
Welcome a shore, a shore.

FOOL
What Mounsieur Musick?

STREMON
My fine Fool.

BOY
Fellow Crack, why what a consort
Are we now blest withal?

FOOL
Fooling and fidling,
Nay and we live not now boys; what new songs, Sirra?

STREMON
A thousand, man, a thousand.

FOOL
Itching Airs
Alluding to the old sport.

STREMON
Of all sizes.

FOOL
And how does small Tym Treble here; the heart on't?

2ND BOY
To do you service.

FOOL
O Tym the times, the times Tym.

STREMON
How does the General,
And next what money's stirring?

CHILAX

For the General
He's here, but such a General!
The time's chang'd, Stremon,
He was the liberal General, and the loving,
The feeder of a Souldier, and the Father,
But now become the stupid'st.

STREMON
Why, what ails he?

CHILAX
Nay, if a Horse knew, and his head's big enough,
I'le hang for't; did'st thou ever see a Dog
Run mad o'th' tooth-ache, such another toy
Is he now, so he glotes and grins, and bites.

FOOL
Why hang him quickly,
And then he cannot hurt folks.

CHILAX
One hour raving,
Another smiling, not a word the third hour,
I tell thee Stremon h'as a stirring soul,
What ever it attempts or labours at
Would wear out twenty bodies in another.

FOOL
I'le keep it out of me, for mine's but Buckram,
He would bownce that out in two hours.

CHILAX
Then he talks
The strangest and the maddest stuff from reason,
Or any thing ye offer; stand thou there,
I'le show thee how he is, for I'le play Memnon
The strangest General that ere thou heardst of, Stremon.

STREMON
My Lord.

CHILAX
Go presently and find me
A black Horse with a blew tail; bid the blank Cornet
Charge through the Sea, and sink the Navy: softly,
Our souls are things not to be waken'd in us
With larums, and loud bawlings, for in Elyzium
Stilness and quietness, and sweetness, Sirra,

I will have, for it much concerns mine honour,
Such a strong reputation for my welcome
As all the world shall say: for in the forefront
So many on white Unicorns, next them
My Gentlemen, my Cavaliers and Captains,
Ten deep and trapt with Tenter-hooks to take hold
Of all occasions: for Friday cannot fish out
The end I aim at; tell me of Diocles,
And what he dares do? dare he meet me naked?
Thunder in this hand? in his left—Fool—

FOOL
Yes, Sir.

CHILAX
Fool, I would have thee fly i'th' Air, fly swiftly
To that place where the Sun sets, there deliver.

FOOL
Deliver? what, Sir?

CHILAX
This Sir, this ye slave, Sir,

[All laugh.

Death ye rude Rogues, ye Scarabe's.

FOOL
Hold for Heav'ns sake, Lieutenant, sweet Lieutenant.

CHILAX
I have done, Sir.

BOY
You have wrung his neck off.

CHILAX
No Boy, 'tis the nature
Of this strange passion when't hits to hale people
Along by th' hair, to kick 'em, break their heads.

FOOL
Do ye call this Acting, was your part to beat me?

CHILAX
Yes, I must act all that he does.

FOOL
Plague act ye,
I'le act no more.

STREMON
'Tis but to shew man.

FOOL
Then man
He should have shew'd it only, and not done it,
I am sure he beat me beyond Action,
Gouts o' your heavy fist.

CHILAX
I'le have thee to him,
Thou hast a fine wit, fine fool, and canst play rarely.
He'l hug thee, Boy, and stroke thee.

FOOL
I'le to the stocks first,
E're I be strok't thus.

STREMON
But how came he, Chilax?

CHILAX
I know not that.

STREMON
I'le to him.

CHILAX
He loves thee well,
And much delights to hear thee sing; much taken
He has been with thy battel songs.

STREMON
If Musick
Can find his madness; I'le so fiddle him,
That out it shall by th' shoulders.

CHILAX
My fine Fidler,
He'l firk you and ye take not heed too: 'twill be rare sport
To see his own trade triumph over him;
His Lute lac'd to his head, for creeping hedges;
For mony there's none stirring; try good Stremon
Now what your silver sound can do; our voices

Are but vain Echoes.

STREMON
Something shall be done
Shall make him understand all; let's toth' Tavern,
I have some few Crowns left yet: my whistle wet once
I'le pipe him such a Paven—

CHILAX
Hold thy head up,
I'le cure it with a quart of wine; come Coxcomb,
Come Boy take heed of Napkins.

FOOL
Youl'd no more acting?

CHILAX
No more Chicken.

FOOL
Go then.

[Exeunt **OMNES**.

[Enter **SIPHAX** at one door, and a **GENTLEMAN** at the other.

SIPHAX
God save you Sir; pray how might I see the Princess?

GENTLEMAN
Why very fitly, Sir, she's even now ready
To walk out this way intoth' Park; stand there,
Ye cannot miss her sight, Sir.

SIPHAX
I much thank ye.

[Exit **GENTLEMAN**.

[Enter **CALIS**, **LUCIPPE**, and **CLEANTHE**.

CALIS
Let's have a care, for I'le assure ye Wenches
I wou'd not meet him willingly again;
For though I do not fear him, yet his fashion
I wou'd not be acquainted much with.

CLEANTHE

Gentle Lady,
Ye need not fear, the walks are view'd and empty,
But me thinks, Madam, this kind heart of his—

LUCIPPE
He's slow a coming.

SIPHAX
Keep me ye blest Angels,
What killing power is this?

CALIS
Why, dost thou look for't?
Dost think he spoke in earnest?

LUCIPPE
Methinks, Madam,
A Gentleman should keep his word; and to a Lady,
A Lady of your excellencies.

CALIS
Out Fool!
Send me his heart? what should we do with't? dance it?

LUCIPPE
Dry it and drink it for the Worms.

CALIS
Who's that?
What man stands there?

CLEANTHE
Where?

CALIS
There.

CLEANTHE
A Gentleman,
Which I beseech your grace to honour so much,
As know him for your servants Brother.

CALIS
Siphax?

CLEANTHE
The same an't please your grace; what does he here?
Upon what business? and I ignorant?

CALIS
He's grown a handsome Gentleman: good Siphax
Y'are welcome from the Wars; wou'd ye with us, Sir?
Pray speak your will: he blushes, be not fearfull,
I can assure ye for your Sisters sake, Sir,
There's my hand on it.

CLEANTHE
Do you hear, Sir?

CALIS
Sure these Souldiers
Are all grown senseless.

CLEANTHE
Do ye know where ye are, Sir?

CALIS
Tongue-tyed,
He looks not well too, by my life, I think—

CLEANTHE
Speak for shame speak.

LUCIPPE
A man wou'd speak—

CALIS
These Souldiers
Are all dumb Saints: consider and take time, Sir,
Let's forward Wenches, come, his Palat's down.

LUCIPPE
Dare these men charge i'th' face of fire and bullets?
And hang their heads down at a handsome Woman?
Good master Mars, that's a foul fault.

[Exit **CALIS** and **LUCIPPE**.

CLEANTHE
Fye beast,
No more my Brother.

SIPHAX
Sister, honoured Sister.

CLEANTHE

Dishonoured fool.

SIPHAX
I do confess.

CLEANTHE
Fye on thee.

SIPHAX
But stay till I deliver.

CLEANTHE
Let me go,
I am asham'd to own thee.

SIPHAX
Fare ye well then,
Ye must ne're see me more.

CLEANTHE
Why stay dear Siphax,
My anger's past; I will hear ye speak.

SIPHAX
O Sister!

CLEANTHE
Out with it Man.

SIPHAX
O I have drunk my mischief.

CLEANTHE
Ha? what?

SIPHAX
My destruction.
In at mine eyes I have drunk it; O the Princess,
The rare sweet Princess!

CLEANTHE
How fool? the rare Princess?
Was it the Princess that thou said'st?

SIPHAX
The Princess.

CLEANTHE

Thou dost not love her sure, thou darst not.

SIPHAX
Yes by Heaven.

CLEANTHE
Yes by Heaven? I know thou darst not.
The Princess? 'tis thy life the knowledge of it,
Presumption that will draw into it all thy kindred,
And leave 'em slaves and succourless; the Princess?
Why she's a sacred thing to see and worship,
Fixt from us as the Sun is, high, and glorious,
To be ador'd not doted on; desire things possible,
Thou foolish young man, nourish not a hope
Will hale thy heart out.

SIPHAX
'Tis my destinie,
And I know both disgrace and death will quit it,
If it be known.

CLEANTHE
Pursue it not then, Siphax,
Get thee good wholesome thoughts may nourish thee,
Go home and pray.

SIPHAX
I cannot.

CLEANTHE
Sleep then, Siphax,
And dream away thy doting.

SIPHAX
I must have her,
Or you no more your Brother; work Cleanthe,
Work, and work speedily, or I shall die Wench.

CLEANTHE
Dye then, I dare forget; farewel.

SIPHAX
Farewel Sister.
Farewel for ever, see me buried.

CLEANTHE
Stay.
Pray stay: he's all my brothers: no way Siphax,

No other Woman?

SIPHAX
None, none, she or sinking.

CLEANTHE
Go and hope well, my life I'le venture for thee
And all my art, a Woman may work miracles;
No more, pray heartily against my fortunes,
For much I fear a main one.

SIPHAX
I shall do it.

[Exeunt.

ACTUS TERTIUS

SCENA PRIMA

Enter a **PRIESTESS** of Venus and a **BOY**.

PRIESTESS
Find him by any means; and good child tell him
He has forgot his old friend, give him this,
And say this night without excuse or business,
As ever he may find a friend, come to me,
He knows the way and how, begon.

BOY
I gallop.

[Exit **BOY**.

[Enter **CLEANTHE**.

CLEANTHE
I have been looking you.

PRIESTESS
The fair Cleanthe,
What may your business be?

CLEANTHE
O holy Mother
Such business, of such strange weight, now or never.

As ye have loved me, as ye do or may do,
When I shall find a fit time.

PRIESTESS
If by my means
Your business may be fitted; ye know me,
And how I am tyed unto you; be bold Daughter
To build your best hopes.

CLEANTHE
O but 'tis a strange one,
Stuck with as many dangers—

PRIESTESS
There's the working,
Small things perform themselves and give no pleasures;
Be confident, through death I'le serve.

CLEANTHE
Here.

PRIESTESS
Fye no corruption.

CLEANTHE
Take it; 'tis yours,
And goodness is no gall to th' Conscience,
I know ye have ways to vent it: ye may hold it.

PRIESTESS
I'll keep it for ye; when?

CLEANTHE
To morrow morning
I'll visit ye again; and when occasion
Offers it self—

PRIESTESS
Instruct me, and have at ye.

CLEANTHE
Farewel till then; be sure.

PRIESTESS
As your own thoughts, Lady.

CLEANTHE
'Tis a main work, and full of fear.

[Exit **CLEANTHE**.

PRIESTESS
Fools only
Make their effects seem fearful, farewell daughter.
This gold was well got for my old tuff Souldier,
Now I shall be his sweet again; what business
Is this she has a foot? some lusty lover
Beyond her line, the young Wench would fain piddle,
A little to revive her must be thought of,
'Tis even so, she must have it; but how by my means,
A Devil, can she drive it? I that wait still
Before the Goddess, giving Oracle,
How can I profit her? 'tis her own project,
And if she cast it false, her own fault be it.

[Exit **PRIESTESS**.

[Enter **POLYDOR, EUMENES, CAPTAINS, STREMON**.

POLYDOR
Why, this is utter madness.

EUMENES
Thus it is, Sir.

POLYDOR
Only the Princess sight?

FIRST CAPTAIN
All we can judge at.

POLYDOR
This must be lookt to timely.

EUMENES
Yes, and wisely.

POLYDOR
He does not offer at his life?

EUMENES
Not yet, Sir,
That we can hear of.

POLYDOR
Noble Gentlemen,

Let me entreat your watches over him,
Ye cannot do a worthier work.

SECOND CAPTAIN
We came, Sir,
Provided for that service.

POLYDOR
Where is Chilax?

STREMON
A little busie, Sir.

POLYDOR
Is the Fool and Boy here?

STREMON
They are, Sir.

[Enter **MEMNON**.

POLYDOR
Let 'em be still so; and as they find his humours.

EUMENES
Now ye may behold him.

POLYDOR
Stand close, and make no noise;
By his eyes now, Gentlemen,
I guess him full of anger.

EUMENES
Be not seen there.

MEMNON
The hour's past long ago, he's false and fearful,
Coward, go with thy Caitive soul, thou Cur Dog,
Thou cold Clod, wild fire warm thee, monstrous fearful,
I know the Slave shakes but to think on't.

POLYDOR
Who's that?

EUMENES
I know not, Sir.

MEMNON

But I shall catch ye, Rascal,
Your mangy Soul is not immortal here, Sir,
Ye must dye, and we must meet; we must, maggot,
Be sure we must, for not a Nook of Hell,
Not the most horrid Pit shall harbour thee;
The Devils tail sha'n't hide thee, but I'll have thee,
And how I'll use thee! whips and firebrands:
Tosting thy tail against a flame of wild fire,
And basting it with Brimstone, shall be nothing,
Nothing at all; I'll teach ye to be treacherous:
Was never Slave so swing'd since Hell was Hell
As I will swinge thy Slaves Soul; and be sure on't.

POLYDOR
Is this imagination, or some circumstance?
For 'tis extream strange.

EUMENES
So is all he does, Sir.

MEMNON
Till then I'll leave ye; who's there? where's the Surgeon?
Demagoras?

DEMAGORAS
My Lord.

MEMNON
Bring the Surgeon:
And wait you too.

[Enter **SURGEON**.

POLYDOR
What wou'd he with a Surgeon?

EUMENES
Things mustring in his head: pray mark.

MEMNON
Come hither,
Have you brought your Instruments?

SURGEON
They are within, Sir.

MEMNON
Put to the doors a while there; ye can incise

To a hairs breadth without defacing.

SURGEON
Yes Sir.

MEMNON
And take out fairly from the flesh.

SURGEON
The least thing.

MEMNON
Well come hither; take off my doublet,
For look ye Surgeon, I must have ye cut
My Heart out here, and handsomly: Nay, stare not,
Nor do not start; I'll cut your throat else, Surgeon,
Come swear to do it.

SURGEON
Good Sir—

MEMNON
Sirrah, hold him,
I'll have but one blow at his head.

SURGEON
I'll do it,
Why what should we do living after you, Sir?
We'll dye before if ye please.

MEMNON
No, no.

SURGEON
Living? hang living.
Is there ne'r a Cat hole where I may creep through?
Would I were in the Indies.

[Aside.

MEMNON
Swear then, and after my death presently
To kill your selves and follow, as ye are honest,
As ye have faiths, and loves to me.

DEMAGORAS
We'll do it.

EUMENES
Pray do not stir yet, we are near enough
To run between all dangers.

MEMNON
Here I am, Sir;
Come, look upon me, view the best way boldly,
Fear nothing, but cut home; if your hand shake, Sirrah,
Or any way deface my heart i'th' cutting,
Make the least scratch upon it; but draw it whole,
Excellent fair, shewing at all points, Surgeon,
The Honour and the Valour of the Owner,
Mixt with the most immaculate love I send it,
Look to't, I'll slice thee to the Soul.

SURGEON
Ne'r fear, Sir,
I'll do it daintily; would I were out once.

MEMNON
I will not have ye smile, Sirrah, when ye do it,
As though ye cut a Ladies Corn; 'tis scurvy:
Do me it as thou dost thy Prayers, seriously.

SURGEON
I'll do it in a dump, Sir.

MEMNON
In a Dog, Sir,
I'll have no dumps, nor dumplins; fetch your tools,
And then I'll tell ye more.

SURGEON
If I return
To hear more, I'll be hang'd for't.

MEMNON
Quick, quick.

DEMAGORAS
Yes Sir,
With all the heels we have.

[Exeunt **SURGEON**, **DEMAGORAS**.

EUMENES
Yet stand.

POLYDOR
He'l do it.

EUMENES
He cannot, and we here.

MEMNON
Why when ye Rascals,
Ye dull Slaves: will ye come, Sir? Surgeon, syringe,
Dog-leach, shall I come fetch ye?

POLYDOR
Now I'll to him.
God save ye honour'd Brother.

MEMNON
My dear Polydor,
Welcome from travel, welcome; and how do ye?

POLYDOR
Well Sir, would you were so.

MEMNON
I am, I thank ye.
You are a better'd man much, I the same still,
An old rude Souldier, Sir.

POLYDOR
Pray be plain, Brother,
And tell me but the meaning of this Vision,
For to me it appears no more; so far
From common Course and Reason.

MEMNON
Thank thee, Fortune,
At length I have found the man: the man must do it,
The man in honour bound.

POLYDOR
To do what?

MEMNON
Hark, for I will bless ye with the circumstance
Of that weak shadow that appear'd.

POLYDOR
Speak on, Sir.

[Walks with him.

MEMNON
It is no Story for all ears.

POLYDOR [Whispers]
The Princess?

MEMNON
Peace and hear all.

POLYDOR
How?

EUMENES
Sure 'tis dangerous
He starts so at it.

POLYDOR
Your heart? do you know, Sir?

MEMNON
Yes, Pray thee be softer.

POLYDOR
Me to do it?

MEMNON
Only reserv'd, and dedicated.

POLYDOR
For shame, Brother,
Know what ye are, a man.

MEMNON
None of your Athens,
Good sweet Sir, no Philosophy, thou feel'st not
The honourable end, fool.

POLYDOR
I am sure I feel
The shame and scorn that follows; have ye serv'd thus long
The glory of your Country, in your Conquests?
The envy of your Neighbours, in your Vertues?
Rul'd Armies of your own, given Laws to Nations,
Belov'd and fear'd as far as Fame has travell'd,
Call'd the most fortunate and happy Memnon,
To lose all here at home, poorly to lose it?

Poorly, and pettishly, ridiculously
To fling away your fortune? where's your Wisedom?
Where's that you govern'd others by, discretion?
Do's your Rule lastly hold upon your self? fie Brother,
How ye are faln? Get up into your honour,
The top branch of your bravery, and from thence,
Look and behold how little Memnon seems now.

MEMNON
Hum! 'tis well spoken; but dost thou think young Scholar,
The tongues of Angels from my happiness
Could turn the end I aim at? no, they cannot.
This is no Book-case, Brother; will ye do it?
Use no more art, I am resolv'd.

POLYDOR
Ye may Sir
Command me to do any thing that's honest,
And for your noble end: but this, it carries—

MEMNON
Ye shall not be so honour'd; live an Ass still,
And learn to spell for profit: go, go study.

EUMENES
Ye must not hold him up so, he is lost then.

MEMNON
Get thee to School again, and talk of turnips,
And find the natural Cause out, why a Dog
Turns thrice about e're he lyes down: there's Learning.

POLYDOR
Come, I will do it now; 'tis brave, I find it,
And now allow the reason.

MEMNON
O do you so, Sir?
Do ye find it currant?

POLYDOR
Yes, yes, excellent.

MEMNON
I told ye.

POLYDOR
I was foolish: I have here too

The rarest way to find the truth out; hark ye?
Ye shall be rul'd by me.

MEMNON
It will be: but—

POLYDOR
I reach it,
If the worst fall, have at the worst; we'll both go.
But two days, and 'tis thus; ha?

MEMNON
'Twill do well so.

POLYDOR
Then is't not excellent, do ye conceive it?

MEMNON
'Twill work for certain.

POLYDOR
O 'twill tickle her,
And you shall know then by a line.

MEMNON
I like it,
But let me not be fool'd again.

POLYDOR
Doubt nothing,
You do me wrong then, get ye in there private
As I have taught ye; Basta.

MEMNON
Work.

[Exit **MEMNON**.

POLYDOR
I will do.

EUMENES
Have ye found the cause?

POLYDOR
Yes, and the strangest, Gentlemen,
That e'r I heard of, anon I'll tell ye: Stremon
Be you still near him to affect his fancy,

And keep his thoughts off: let the Fool and Boy
Stay him, they may do some pleasure too: Eumenes
What if he had a Wench, a handsome Whore brought,
Rarely drest up, and taught to state it?

EUMENES
Well Sir.

POLYDOR
His cause is meerly heat: and made believe
It were the Princess mad for him.

EUMENES
I think
'Twere not amiss.

FIRST CAPTAIN
And let him kiss her.

POLYDOR
What else?

SECOND CAPTAIN
I'll be his Bawd an't please you, young and wholesome
I can assure ye he shall have.

EUMENES
Faith let him.

POLYDOR
He shall, I hope 'twill help him, walk a little.
I'll tell you how his case stands, and my project
In which you may be mourners, but by all means
Stir not you from him, Stremon.

STREMON
On our lives, Sir.

[Exeunt.

[Enter **PRIESTESS** and **CHILAX**.

PRIESTESS
O y'are a precious man! two days in town
And never see your old Friend?

CHILAX
Prithee pardon me.

PRIESTESS
And in my Conscience if I had not sent.

CHILAX
No more, I would ha' come; I must.

PRIESTESS
I find ye,
God a mercy want, ye never care for me
But when your Slops are empty.

CHILAX
Ne'r fear that, Wench;
Shall find good currant Coin still; Is this the old House?

PRIESTESS
Have ye forgot it?

CHILAX
And the door still standing
That goes into the Temple?

PRIESTESS
Still.

CHILAX
The Robes too,
That I was wont to shift in here?

PRIESTESS
All here still.

CHILAX
O ye tuff Rogue, what troubles have I trotted through!
What fears and frights! every poor Mouse a Monster
That I heard stir, and every stick I trod on,
A sharp sting to my Conscience.

PRIESTESS
'Las poor Conscience.

CHILAX
And all to liquor thy old Boots, Wench.

PRIESTESS
Out Beast:
How you talk!

CHILAX
I am old, Wench,
And talking to an old man is like a stomacher,
It keeps his blood warm.

PRIESTESS
But pray tell me—

CHILAX
Any thing.

PRIESTESS
Where did the Boy meet with ye? at a Wench sure?
At one end of a Wench, a Cup of Wine, sure?

CHILAX
Thou know'st I am too honest.

PRIESTESS
That's your fault,
And that the Surgeon knows.

CHILAX
Then farewel,
I will not fail ye soon.

PRIESTESS
Ye shall stay Supper;
I have sworn ye shall, by this ye shall.

CHILAX
I will, Wench;
But after Supper for an hour, my business.

PRIESTESS
And but an hour?

CHILAX
No by this kiss, that ended
I will return and all night in thine Arms wench.

PRIESTESS
No more, I'le take your meaning; come 'tis Supper time.

[Exeunt.

[Enter **CALIS, CLEANTHE, LUCIPPE**.

CALIS
Thou art not well.

CLEANTHE
Your grace sees more a great deal
Than I feel, (yet I lye) O Brother!

CALIS
Mark her,
Is not the quickness of her eye consumed, wench?
The lively red and white?

LUCIPPE
Nay she is much alter'd,
That on my understanding, all her sleeps Lady
Which were as sound and sweet—

CLEANTHE
Pray do not force me,
Good Madam, where I am not, to be ill,
Conceit's a double sickness; on my faith your highness
Is meer mistaken in me.

[A Dead March within of Drum and Sagbutts.

CALIS
I am glad on't.
Yet this I have ever noted when thou wast thus,
It still forerun some strange event: my Sister
Died when thou wast thus last: hark hark, ho,
What mournfull noise is this comes creeping forward?
Still it grows nearer, nearer, do ye hear it?

[Enter **POLYDOR** and **CAPTAINS**, **EUMENES** mourning.

LUCIPPE
It seems some Souldiers funeral: see it enters.

CALIS
What may it mean?

POLYDOR
The Gods keep ye fair Calis.

CALIS
This man can speak, and well; he stands and views us;
Wou'd I were ne'r worse look't upon: how humbly

His eyes are cast now to the Earth! pray mark him
And mark how rarely he has rankt his troubles:
See now he weeps, they all weep; a sweeter sorrow
I never look't upon, nor one that braver
Became his grief; your will with us?

POLYDOR
Great Lady,

[Plucks out the Cup.

Excellent beauty.

CALIS
He speaks handsomely.
What a rare rhetorician his grief plaies!
That stop was admirable.

POLYDOR
See, see thou Princess,
Thou great commander of all hearts.

CALIS
I have found it,
O how my soul shakes!

POLYDOR
See, see the noble heart
Of him that was the noblest: see and glory
(Like the proud God himself) in what thou hast purchas'd,
Behold the heart of Memnon: does it start ye?

CALIS
Good gods, what has his wildness done?

POLYDOR
Look boldlie,
You boldlie said you durst, look wretched woman,
Nay flie not back fair follie, 'tis too late now,
Vertue and blooming honour bleed to death here,
Take it, the Legacie of Love bequeath'd ye,
Of cruel Love a cruel Legacie;
What was the will that wrought it then? can ye weep?
Imbalm it in your truest tears
If women can weep a truth, or ever sorrow sunk yet
Into the soul of your sex, for 'tis a Jewel
The worlds worth cannot weigh down,
Take it Lady; And with it all (I dare not curse) my sorrows,

And may they turn to Serpents.

EUMENES
How she looks
Still upon him! see now a tear steals from her.

SECOND CAPTAIN
But still she keeps her eye firm.

POLYDOR
Next read this,
But since I see your spirit somewhat troubled
I'le doe it for ye.

SECOND CAPTAIN
Still she eyes him mainlie.
Goe happy heart for thou shalt lye
Intomb'd in her for whom I dye
Example of her cruelty.
Tell her if she chance to chide
Me for slowness in her pride
That it was for her I died.
If a tear escape her eye
'Tis not for my memory
But thy rights of obsequy.
The Altar was my loving breast,
My heart the sacrificed beast,
And I was my self the Priest.
Your body was the sacred shrine,
Your cruel mind the power divine
Pleas'd with hearts of men, not kine.

EUMENES
Now it pours down.

POLYDOR
I like it rarelie: Ladie.

EUMENES
How greedily she swallows up his language!

SECOND CAPTAIN
Her eye inhabits on him.

POLYDOR
Cruel Ladie,
Great as your beautie scornfull; had your power
But equal poise on all hearts, all hearts perish't;

But Cupid has more shafts than one, more flames too,
And now he must be open ey'd, 'tis Justice:
Live to injoy your longing; live and laugh at
The losses and the miseries we suffer;
Live to be spoken when your crueltie
Has cut off all the vertue from this Kingdom,
Turn'd honour into earth, and faithful service.

CALIS

I swear his anger's excellent.

POLYDOR

Truth, and most tried love
Into disdain and downfall.

CALIS

Still more pleasing.

POLYDOR

Live then I say famous for civil slaughters,
Live and lay out your triumphs, gild your glories,
Live and be spoken this is she, this Ladie,
This goodly Ladie, yet most killing beautie;
This with the two edg'd eyes, the heart for hardness
Outdoing rocks; and coldness, rocks of Crystal.
This with the swelling soul, more coy of Courtship
Than the proud sea is when the shores embrace him;
Live till the mothers find ye, read your story,
And sow their barren curses on your beauty,
Till those that have enjoy'd their loves despise ye,
Till Virgins pray against ye, old age find ye,
And even as wasted coals glow in their dying,
So may the Gods reward ye in your ashes:
But y'are the Sister of my King; more prophecies
Else I should utter of ye, true loves and loyal
Bless themselves ever from ye: so I leave ye.

CALIS

Prethee be angry still young man: good fair Sir
Chide me again, what wou'd this man doe pleas'd,
That in his passion can bewitch souls? stay.

EUMENES

Upon my life she loves him.

CALIS

Pray stay.

POLYDOR
No.

CALIS
I do command ye.

POLYDOR
No, ye cannot Ladie,
I have a spell against ye, Faith and Reason,
Ye are too weak to reach me: I have a heart too,
But not for hawks meat Ladie.

CALIS
Even for Charity
Leave me not thus afflicted: you can teach me.

POLYDOR
How can you Preach that Charity to others
That in your own soul are an Atheist,
Believing neither power nor fear? I trouble ye,
The Gods be good unto ye.

CALIS
Amen.

LUCIPPE
Ladie.

[She Swoons.

CLEANTHE
O royal Madam, Gentlemen for heaven sake.

[They come.

POLYDOR
Give her fresh air, she comes again: away sirs

[They back away.

And here stand close till we perceive the working.

EUMENES
Ye have undone all.

POLYDOR
So I fear.

SECOND CAPTAIN
She loves ye.

EUMENES
And then all hopes lost this way.

POLYDOR
Peace she rises.

CLEANTHE
Now for my purpose Fortune.

CALIS
Where's the Gentleman?

LUCIPPE
Gone Madam.

CALIS
Why gone?

LUCIPPE
H'as dispatch't his business.

CALIS
He came to speak with me,
He did.

CLEANTHE
He did not.

CALIS
For I had many questions.

LUCIPPE
On my Faith Madam, he
Talk't a great while to ye.

CALIS
Thou conceiv'st not,
He talk't not as he should doe; O my heart
Away with that sad sight; didst thou e're love me?

LUCIPPE
Why do you make that question?

CALIS
If thou didst

Run, run wench, run: nay see how thou stir'st.

LUCIPPE
Whither?

CALIS
If 'twere for any thing to please thy self
Thou woud'st run toth' devil: but I am grown—

CLEANTHE
Fie Lady.

CALIS
I ask none of your fortunes, nor your loves,
None of your bent desires I slack, ye are not
In love with all men, are ye? one for shame
You will leave your honour'd mistris? why do ye stare so?
What is that ye see about me, tell me?
Lord what am I become? I am not wilde sure,
Heaven keep that from me: O Cleanthe help me,
Or I am sunk to death.

CLEANTHE
Ye have offended and mightily, love is incenst against ye,
And therefore take my Counsel, to the Temple,
For that's the speediest physick: before the Goddess
Give your repentant prayers: ask her will,
And from the Oracle attend your sentence,
She is milde and mercifull.

CALIS
I will: O Venus
Even as thou lov'st thy self!

CLEANTHE
Now for my fortune.

[Exeunt **CALIS** and **WOMEN**.

POLYDOR
What shall I doe?

FIRST CAPTAIN
Why make your self.

POLYDOR
I dare not,
No Gentlemen, I dare not be a villain,

Though her bright beauty would entice an Angel.
I will toth' King my last hope: get him a woman
As we before concluded: and as ye pass
Give out the Spartans are in arms; and terrible;
And let some letters to that end be feign'd too
And sent to you, some Posts too, to the General;
And let me work: be ne're him still.

EUMENES
We will Sir.

POLYDOR
Farewel: and pray for all: what e're I will ye
Doe it, and hope a fair end.

EUMENES
The Gods speed ye.

[Exeunt.

[Enter **STREMON**, **FOOL**, **BOY** and **SERVANTS**.

SERVANTS
He lies quiet.

STREMON
Let him lye, and as I told ye
Make ready for this shew: h'as divers times
Been calling upon Orpheus to appear
And shew the joyes: now I will be that Orpheus,
And as I play and sing, like beasts and trees
I wou'd have you shap't and enter: thou a Dog, fool,
I have sent about your sutes: the Boy a bush,
An Ass you, you a Lion.

FOOL
I a Dog?
I'le fit you for a Dog. Bow wow.

STREMON
'Tis excellent,
Steal in and make no noise.

FOOL
Bow wow.

STREMON
Away Rogue.

[Exeunt.

[Enter **PRIESTESS** and **CHILAX**.

PRIESTESS
Good sweet friend be not long.

CHILAX
Thou think'st each hour ten
Till I be ferreting.

PRIESTESS
You know I love ye.

CHILAX
I will not be above an hour; let thy robe be readie
And the door be kept.

[**CLEANTHE** knocks within.

PRIESTESS
Who knocks there?
Yet more business?

[Enter **CLEANTHE**.

CHILAX
Have ye more pensioners? the Princess woman?
Nay then I'le stay a little, what game's a foot now?

CLEANTHE
Now is the time.

CHILAX
A rank bawd by this hand too,
She grinds o' both sides: hey boyes.

PRIESTESS
How, your Brother Siphax?
Loves he the Princess?

CLEANTHE
Deadlie, and you know
He is a Gentleman descended noblie.

CHILAX
But a rank knave as ever pist.

CLEANTHE
Hold Mother,
Here's more gold and some jewells.

CHILAX
Here's no villany,
I am glad I came toth' hearing.

PRIESTESS
Alas Daughter,
What would ye have me doe?

CHILAX
Hold off ye old whore;
There's more gold coming; all's mine, all.

CLEANTHE
Do ye shrink now,
Did ye not promise faithfully, and told me
Through any danger?

PRIESTESS
Any I can wade through.

CLEANTHE
Ye shall and easily, the sin not seen neither,
Here's for a better stole and a new vail mother:
Come, ye shall be my friend.

CHILAX
If all hit, hang me,
I'le make ye richer than the Goddess.

PRIESTESS
Say then,
I am yours, what must I doe?

CLEANTHE
I'th' morning
But very early, will the Princess visit
The Temple of the Goddess, being troubled
With strange things that distract her: from the Oracle
(Being strongly too in love) she will demand
The Goddess pleasure, and a Man to cure her,
That Oracle you give: describe my Brother,
You know him perfectly.

PRIESTESS
I have seen him often.

CLEANTHE
And charge her take the next man she shall meet with
When she comes out: you understand me.

PRIESTESS
Well.

CLEANTHE
Which shall be he attending; this is all,
And easily without suspicion ended,
Nor none dare disobey, 'tis Heaven that does it,
And who dares cross it then, or once suspect it?
The venture is most easie.

PRIESTESS
I will doe it.

CLEANTHE
As ye shall prosper?

PRIESTESS
As I shall prosper.

CLEANTHE
Take this too, and farewel; but first hark hither.

CHILAX
What a young whore's this to betray her Mistris?
A thousand Cuckolds shall that Husband be,
That marries thee, thou art so mischievous.
I'le put a spoak among your wheels.

CLEANTHE
Be constant.

PRIESTESS
'Tis done.

CHILAX
I'le doe no more at drop shot then.

[Exit **CHILAX**.

PRIESTESS
FarewelL wench.

[Exeunt **PRIESTESS** and **CLEANTHE**.

Enter a **SERVANT** and **STREMON** at the door.

SERVANT
He stirs, he stirs.

STREMON
Let him, I am ready for him,
He shall not this day perish, if his passions
May be fed with Musick; are they ready?

[Enter **MEMNON**.

SERVANT
All, all: see where he comes.

STREMON
I'le be straight for him.

[Exit **STREMON**.

[Enter **EUMENES** and **CAPTAINS**.

SERVANT
How sad he looks and sullen!

[Stands close.

Here are the Captains: my fear's past now.

MEMNON
Put case i'th' other world
She do not love me neither? I am old 'tis certain.

EUMENES
His spirit is a little quieter.

MEMNON
My blood lost, and limbs stiff; my embraces
Like the cold stubborn bark, hoarie, and heatless,

My words worse: my fame only and atchievements
Which are my strength, my blood, my youth, my fashion,
Must wooe her, win her, wed her; that's but wind,
And women are not brought to bed with shadows:
I do her wrong, much wrong; she is young and blessed,
Sweet as the spring, and as his blossoms tender,
And I a nipping North-wind, my head hung
With hails, and frostie Isicles: are the souls so too
When they depart hence, lame and old, and loveless?
No sure, 'tis ever youth there; Time and Death
Follow our flesh no more: and that forc'd opinion
That spirits have no sexes, I believe not.

[Enter **STREMON**, like Orpheus.

There must be love, there is love: what art thou?

[**SONG**.

STREMON
Orpheus I am, come from the deeps below,
To thee fond man the plagues of love to show:
To the fair fields where loves eternal dwell
There's none that come, but first they pass through hell:
Hark and beware unless thou hast lov'd ever,
Belov'd again, thou shalt see those joyes never.

Hark how they groan that dy'd despairing,
O take heed then:
Hark how they howl for over-daring,
All these were men.

They that be fools, and dye for fame
They lose their name;
And they that bleed
Hark how they speed.

Now in cold frosts, now scorching fires
They sit, and curse their lost desires:
Nor shall these souls be free from pains and fears,
Till Women waft them over in their tears.

MEMNON
How should I know my passage is deni'd me?
Or which of all the Devils dare?

EUMENES
This Song

Was rarely form'd to fit him.

[**SONG**.

ORPHEUS
Charon O Charon,
Thou wafter of the souls to bliss or bane.

CHARON
Who calls the Ferry-man of Hell?

ORPHEUS
Come near,
And say who lives in joy, and who in fear.

CHARON
Those that dye well, Eternal joy shall follow;
Those that dye ill, their own foul fate shall swallow.

ORPHEUS
Shall thy black Bark those guilty spirits stow
That kill themselves for love?

CHARON
O no, no,
My cordage cracks when such great sins are near,
No wind blows fair, nor I myself can stear.

ORPHEUS
What lovers pass and in Elyzium raign?

CHARON
Those Gentle loves that are belov'd again.

ORPHEUS
This Souldier loves, and fain wou'd dye to win,
Shall he goe on?

CHARON
No 'tis too foul a sin.
He must not come aboard: I dare not row,
Storms of despair, and guilty blood will blow.

ORPHEUS
Shall time release him, say?

CHARON
No, no, no, no.

Nor time nor death can alter us, nor prayer;
My boat is destinie, and who then dare
But those appointed come aboard? Live still,
And love by reason, Mortal, not by will.

ORPHEUS
And when thy Mistris shall close up thine eyes,

CHARON
Then come aboard and pass,

ORPHEUS
Till when be wise.

CHARON
Till when be wise.

EUMENES
How still he sits: I hope this Song has setled him.

FIRST CAPTAIN
He bites his lip, and rowles his fiery eyes, yet
I fear for all this—

SECOND CAPTAIN
Stremon still apply to him.

STREMON
Give me more room, sweetly strike, divinely
Such strains as old earth moves at.

ORPHEUS
The power I have over both beast and plant,
Thou man alone feelst miserable want.

[Musick.

Strike you rare Spirits that attend my will,
And lose your savage wildness by my skill.

[Enter a **MASK of BEASTS**.

This Lion was a man of War that died,
As thou wouldst do, to gild his Ladies pride:
This Dog a fool that hung himself for love:
This Ape with daily hugging of a glove,
Forgot to eat and died. This goodly tree,
An usher that still grew before his Ladie,

Wither'd at root. This, for he could not wooe,
A grumbling Lawyer: this pyed Bird a page,
That melted out because he wanted age.
Still these lye howling on the Stygian shore,
O love no more, O love no more.

[Exit **MEMNON**.

EUMENES
He steals off silently, as though he would sleep,
No more, but all be near him, feed his fancie
Good Stremon still; this may lock up his follie.
Yet Heaven knows I much fear him; away softly.

[Exeunt **CAPTAINS**.

FOOL
Did I not doe most doggedly?

STREMON
Most rarelie.

FOOL
He's a brave man, when shall we dog again?

BOY
Unty me first for Gods sake,

FOOL
Help the Boy; he's in a wood poor child: good hony Stremon
Let's have a bear-baiting; ye shall see me play
The rarest for a single Dog: at head all;
And if I do not win immortal glorie,
Play Dog play Devil.

STREMON
Peace for this time.

FOOL
Prethee
Let's sing him a black Santis, then let's all howl
In our own beastly voices; tree keep your time,
Untye there; bow, wow, wow.

STREMON
Away ye Asse, away.

FOOL

Why let us doe something
To satisfie the Gentleman, he's mad;
A Gentleman-like humour, and in fashion,
And must have men as mad about him.

STREMON
Peace,
And come in quicklie, 'tis ten to one else
He'l find a staff to beat a dog; no more words,
I'le get ye all imployment; soft, soft in all.

[Exeunt.

[Enter **CHILAX** and **CLOE**.

CHILAX
When camest thou over wench?

CLOE
But now this evening,
And have been ever since looking out Siphax,
I'th' wars he would have lookt me: sure h'as gotten
Some other Mistris?

CHILAX
A thousand, wench, a thousand,
They are as common here as Caterpillers
Among the corn, they eat up all the Souldiers.

CLOE
Are they so hungry? yet by their leave Chilax,
I'le have a snatch too.

CHILAX
Dost thou love him still wench?

CLOE
Why should I not? he had my Maiden-head
And all my youth.

CHILAX
Thou art come the happiest,
In the most blessed time, sweet wench the fittest,
If thou darst make thy fortune: by this light, Cloe,
And so I'le kiss thee: and if thou wilt but let me,
For 'tis well worth a kindness.

CLOE

What shou'd I let ye?

CHILAX
Enjoy thy miniken.

CLOE
Thou art still old Chilax.

CHILAX
Still still, and ever shall be: if, I say,
Thou wo't strike the stroke: I cannot do much harm wench.

CLOE
Nor much good.

CHILAX
Siphax shall be thy Husband,
Thy very Husband woman, thy fool, thy Cuckold,
Or what thou wilt make him: I am over joy'd,
Ravisht, clean ravisht with this fortune; kiss me,
Or I shall lose my self.

CLOE
My Husband said ye?

CHILAX
Said I? and will say, Cloe: nay and do it
And do it home too; Peg thee as close to him
As birds are with a pin to one another;
I have it, I can do it: thou wantst clothes too,
And hee'l be hang'd unless he marry thee
E're he maintain thee: now he has Ladies, Courtiers
More than his back can bend at, multitudes;
We are taken up for threshers, will ye bite?

CLOE
Yes.

CHILAX
And let me—

CLOE
Yes and let ye—

CHILAX
What!

CLOE

Why that ye wote of.

CHILAX
I cannot stay, take your instructions
And something toward houshold, come, what ever
I shall advise ye, follow it exactlie,
And keep your times I point ye; for I'le tell ye
A strange way you must wade through.

CLOE
Fear not me Sir.

CHILAX
Come then, and let's dispatch this modicum,
For I have but an hour to stay, a short one,
Besides more water for another mill,
An old weak over-shot I must provide for,
There's an old Nunnerie at hand.

CLOE
What's that?

CHILAX
A bawdie house.

CLOE
A pox consume it.

CHILAX
If the stones 'tis built on
Were but as brittle as the flesh lives in it,
Your curse came handsomlie: fear not, there's ladies,
And other good sad people: your pinkt Citizens
Think it no shame to shake a sheet there: Come wench.

[Exeunt.

[Enter **CLEANTHE** and **SIPHAX**.

CLEANTHE
A Souldier and so fearfull?

SIPHAX
Can ye blame me;
When such a weight lies on me?

CLEANTHE
Fye upon ye,

I tell ye, ye shall have her: have her safelie,
And for your wife with her own will.

SIPHAX
Good Sister—

CLEANTHE
What a distrustfull man are you! to morrow,
To morrow morning—

SIPHAX
Is it possible?
Can there be such a happiness?

CLEANTHE
Why hang me
If then ye be not married: if to morrow night,
Ye doe not—

SIPHAX
O dear Sister—

CLEANTHE
What ye wou'd doe,
What ye desire to doe; lie with her: Devil,
What a dull man are you!

SIPHAX
Nay I believe now,
And shall she love me?

CLEANTHE
As her life, and stroke ye.

SIPHAX
O I will be her Servant.

CLEANTHE
'Tis your dutie.

SIPHAX
And she shall have her whole will.

CLEANTHE
Yes 'tis reason,
She is a Princess, and by that rule boundless.

SIPHAX

What wou'd you be? for I wou'd have ye Sister
Chuse some great place about us: as her woman
Is not so fit.

CLEANTHE
No, no, I shall find places.

SIPHAX
And yet to be a Ladie of her bed-chamber,
I hold not so fit neither,
Some great title, believe it, shall be look't out.

CLEANTHE
Ye may, a Dutchess
Or such a toye, a small thing pleases me Sir.

SIPHAX
What you will Sister: if a neighbour Prince,
When we shall come to raign—

CLEANTHE
We shall think on't,
Be ready at the time, and in that place too,
And let me work the rest, within this half hour
The Princess will be going, 'tis almost morning,
Away and mind your business.

SIPHAX
Fortune bless us.

[Exeunt.

[Enter **KING**, **POLYDOR** and **LORDS**.

POLYDOR
I do beseech your grace to banish me.

KING
Why Gentleman, is she not worthy marriage?

POLYDOR
Most worthy, Sir, where worth again shall meet her,
But I like thick clouds sailing slow and heavy,
Although by her drawn higher, yet shall hide her,
I dare not be a traitor; and 'tis treason,
But to imagine: as you love your honour—

KING

'Tis her first maiden doting, and if crost,
I know it kills her.

FIRST LORD
How knows your grace she loves him?

KING
Her woman told me all (beside his story)
Her maid Lucippe, on what reason too,
And 'tis beyond all but enjoying.

POLYDOR
Sir,
Even by your wisdom; by that great discretion
Ye owe to rule and order—

SECOND LORD
This man's mad sure,
To plead against his fortune—

FIRST LORD
And the King too,
Willing to have it so!

POLYDOR
By those dead Princes
From whose descents ye stand a star admir'd at,
Lay not so base a lay upon your vertues;
Take heed, for honours sake take heed: the bramble
No wise man ever planted by the rose,
It cankers all her beauty; nor the vine
When her full blushes court the sun, dares any
Choke up with wanton Ivy: good my Lords,
Who builds a monument, the Basis Jasper,
And the main body Brick?

SECOND LORD
Ye wrong your worth,
Ye are a Gentleman descended nobly.

FIRST LORD
In both bloods truly noble.

KING
Say ye were not,
My will can make ye so.

POLYDOR

No, never, never;
'Tis not descent, nor will of Princes does it,
'Tis Vertue which I want, 'tis Temperance,
Man, honest man: is't fit your Majesty
Should call my drunkenness, my rashness, Brother?
Or such a blessed Maid my breach of faith,
(For I am most lascivious) and fell angers
In which I am also mischievous, her Husband?
O Gods preserve her! I am wild as Winter,
Ambitious as the Devil: out upon me,
I hate my self, Sir, if ye dare bestow her
Upon a Subject, ye have one deserves her.

KING
But him she does not love: I know your meaning.
This young mans love unto his noble Brother
Appears a mirrour; what must now be done Lords?
For I am gravel'd, if she have not him,
She dies for certain, if his Brother miss her,
Farewel to him, and all our honours.

FIRST LORD
He is dead, Sir,
Your Grace has heard of that, and strangely.

KING
No,
I can assure you no, there was a trick in't,
Read that, and then know all; what ails the Gentleman?
Hold him; how do ye Sir?

[**POLYDOR** is sick o'th' sudden.

POLYDOR
Sick o'th' sudden,
Extreamly ill, wondrous ill.

KING
Where did it take ye?

POLYDOR
Here in my head, Sir, and my heart, for Heaven sake.

KING
Conduct him to his Chamber presently,
And bid my Doctors—

POLYDOR

No, I shall be well, Sir,
I do beseech your Grace, even for the Gods sake
Remember my poor Brother, I shall pray then.

KING
Away, he grows more weak still: I will do it,
Or Heaven forget me ever. Now your Counsels,

[Exit **POLYDOR**.

For I am at my wits end; what with you Sir?

[Enter **MESSENGER** with a Letter.

MESSENGER
Letters from warlike Pelius.

KING
Yet more troubles?
The Spartans are in Arms, and like to win all:
Supplies are sent for, and the General;
This is more cross than t'other; come let's to him,
For he must have her, 'tis necessity,
Or we must lose our honours, let's plead all,
For more than all is needful, shew all reason
If love can hear o' that side, if she yield
We have fought best, and won the noblest field.

[Exeunt.

[Enter **EUMENES, CAPTAINS, STREMON**.

FIRST CAPTAIN
I have brought the wench, a lusty wench,
And somewhat like the Princess.

EUMENES
'Tis the better, let's see her,
And go you in and tell him, that her Grace
Is come to visit him: how sleeps he Stremon?

STREMON
He cannot, only thinks, and calls on Polydor,
Swears he will not be fool'd; sometimes he rages,
And sometimes sits and muses.

[Exit **STREMON**.

[Enter **WHORE** and **CAPTAIN**.

EUMENES
He's past all help sure?
How do ye like her?

SECOND CAPTAIN
By th' mass a good round Virgin,
And at first sight resembling, she is well cloath'd too.

EUMENES
But is she sound?

SECOND CAPTAIN
Of wind and limb, I warrant her.

EUMENES
You are instructed Lady?

WHORE
Yes, and know, Sir,
How to behave my self, ne're fear.

EUMENES
Polybius,
Where did he get this Vermin?

FIRST CAPTAIN
Hang him Badger,
There's not a hole free from him, whores and whores mates
Do all pay him obedience.

EUMENES
Indeed i'th' War,
His quarter was all Whore, Whore upon Whore,
And lin'd with Whore; beshrew me 'tis a fair Whore.

FIRST CAPTAIN
She has smockt away her blood; but fair or foul,
Or blind or lame, that can but lift her leg up,
Comes not amiss to him, he rides like a night Mare,
All Ages, all Religions.

EUMENES
Can ye state it?

WHORE
I'le make a shift.

EUMENES
He must lie with ye, Lady.

WHORE
Let him, he's not the first man I have lain with,
Nor shall not be the last.

[Enter **MEMNON**.

SECOND CAPTAIN
He comes, no more words,
She has her lesson throughly; how he views her!

EUMENES
Go forward now, so, bravely, stand!

MEMNON
Great Lady,
How humbly I am bound—

WHORE
You shall not kneel, Sir,
Come, I have done you wrong; stand my Souldier,
And thus I make amends—

[Kisses him.

EUMENES
A Plague confound ye,
Is this your state?

SECOND CAPTAIN
'Tis well enough.

MEMNON
O Lady,
Your Royal hand, your hand my dearest beauty
Is more than I must purchase: here divine one,
I dare revenge my wrongs: ha?

FIRST CAPTAIN
A damn'd foul one.

EUMENES
The Lees of Baudy prewns: mourning Gloves?
All spoil'd by Heaven.

MEMNON
Ha! who art thou?

SECOND CAPTAIN
A shame on ye,
Ye clawing scabby Whore.

MEMNON
I say, who art thou?

EUMENES
Why 'tis the Princess, Sir.

MEMNON
The Devil, Sir,
'Tis some Roguey thing.

WHORE
If this abuse be love, Sir,
Or I that laid aside my modesty—

EUMENES
So far thou't never find it.

MEMNON
Do not weep,
For if ye be the Princess, I will love ye,
Indeed I will, and honour ye, fight for ye,
Come, wipe your eyes; by Heaven she stinks; who art thou?
Stinks like a poyson'd Rat behind a hanging?
Woman, who art? like a rotten Cabbage.

SECOND CAPTAIN
Y'are much to blame, Sir, 'tis the Princess.

MEMNON
How?
She the Princess?

EUMENES
And the loving Princess.

FIRST CAPTAIN
Indeed the doating Princess.

MEMNON
Come hither once more,
The Princess smells like mornings breath, pure Amber,

Beyond the courted Indies in her spices.
Still a dead Rat by Heaven; thou a Princess?

EUMENES
What a dull Whore is this!

MEMNON
I'le tell ye presently,
For if she be a Princess, as she may be
And yet stink too, and strongly, I shall find her;
Fetch the Numidian Lyon I brought over,
If she be sprung from the Royal blood, the Lyon,
He'l do you reverence, else—

WHORE
I beseech your Lordship—

EUMENES
He'l tear her all to pieces.

WHORE
I am no Princess, Sir.

MEMNON
Who brought thee hither?

SECOND CAPTAIN
If ye confess, we'll hang ye.

WHORE
Good my Lord—

MEMNON
Who art thou then?

WHORE
A poor retaining Whore, Sir,
To one of your Lordships Captains.

MEMNON
Alas poor Whore,
Go, be a Whore still, and stink worse: Ha, ha, ha.

[Exit **WHORE**.

What fools are these, and Coxcombs!

[Exit **MEMNON**.

EUMENES
I am right glad yet,
He takes it with such lightness.

FIRST CAPTAIN
Me thinks his face too
Is not so clouded as it was; how he looks!

EUMENES
Where's your dead Rat?

SECOND CAPTAIN
The Devil dine upon her
Loins; why what a Medicine had he gotten
To try a Whore!

[Enter **STREMON**.

STREMON
Here's one from Polydor stays to speak with ye.

EUMENES
With whom?

STREMON
With all; where has the General been?
He's laughing to himself extreamly.

EUMENES
Come,
I'le tell thee how; I am glad yet he's so merry.

[Exeunt.

ACTUS QUINTUS

SCENA PRIMA

Enter **CHILAX** and **PRIESTESS, CALIS, LADY** and **NUN**.

CHILAX
What lights are those that enter there, still nearer?
Plague o' your rotten itch, do you draw me hither
Into the Temple to betray me? was there no place
To satisfie your sin in? Gods forgive me,

Still they come forward.

PRIESTESS
Peace ye fool, I have found it,
'Tis the young Princess Calis.

CHILAX
'Tis the Devil,
To claw us for our catterwawling.

PRIESTESS [To **CHILAX**]
Retire softly,
I did not look for you these two hours, Lady,
Beshrew your hast: that way.

CHILAX
That goes to the Altar!
Ye old blind Beast.

PRIESTESS
I know not, any way;
Still they come nearer,
I'le in to th' Oracle.

CHILAX
That's well remembred I'le in with ye.

PRIESTESS
Do.

[Exeunt **PRIESTESS** and **CHILAX**.

[Enter **CALIS** and her **TRAIN** with lights, singing: **LUCIPPE**, **CLEANTHE**.

[**SONG**
O fair sweet Goddess Queen of Loves,
Soft and gentle, as thy Doves,
Humble ey'd, and ever ruing
Those poor hearts, their Loves pursuing:
O thou Mother of delights,
Crowner of all happy nights,
Star of dear content, and pleasure,
Of mutual loves the endless treasure,
Accept this sacrifice we bring,
Thou continual youth and Spring,
Grant this Lady her desires,
And every hour we'll crown thy fires.

[Enter a **NUN**.

Nun. You about her all retire,
Whilest the Princess feeds the fire,
When your Devotions ended be
To the Oracle I will attend ye.

[Exit **NUN** and draws the Curtain close to **CALIS**.

[Enter **STREMON** and **EUMENES**.

STREMON
He will abroad.

EUMENES
How does his humour hold him?

STREMON
He is now grown wondrous sad, weeps often too,
Talks of his Brother to himself, starts strangely.

EUMENES
Does he not curse?

STREMON
No.

EUMENES
Nor break out in fury,
Offering some new attempt?

STREMON
Neither; to th' Temple
Is all we hear of now: what there he will do—

EUMENES
I hope repent his folly, let's be near him.

STREMON
Where are the rest?

EUMENES
About a business
Concerns him mainly, if Heav'n cure his madness,
He's made for ever, Stremon.

STREMON
Does the King know it?

EUMENES
Yes, and much troubled with it, he's now gone
To seek his Sister out.

STREMON
Come let's away then.

[Exeunt **EUMENES**.

STREMON
Calis.

[Enter **NUN**, she opens the Curtain to **CALIS**. **CALIS** at the Oracle.

NUN
Peace to your Prayers Lady, will it please ye
To pass on to the Oracle?

CALIS
Most humbly.

[**CHILAX** and **PRIESTESS**, in the Oracle.

CHILAX
Do ye hear that?

PRIESTESS
Yes, lie close.

CHILAX
A wildfire take ye,
What shall become of me? I shall be hang'd now:
Is this a time to shake? a halter shake ye,
Come up and juggle, come.

PRIESTESS
I am monstrous fearful.

CHILAX
Up ye old gaping Oyster, up and answer;
A mouldy Mange upon your chops, ye told me
I was safe here till the Bell rung.

PRIESTESS
I was prevented,
And did not look these three hours for the Princess.

CHILAX
Shall we be taken?

PRIESTESS
Speak for loves sake, Chilax;
I cannot, nor I dare not.

CHILAX
I'le speak Treason, for I had as lieve be hang'd for that.

PRIESTESS
Good Chilax.

CHILAX
Must it be sung or said? what shall I tell 'em?
They are here; here now preparing.

PRIESTESS
O my Conscience!

CHILAX
Plague o' your spurgall'd Conscience, does it tire now?
Now when it should be tuffest? I could make thee—

PRIESTESS
Save us, we are both undone else.

CHILAX
Down ye Dog then,
Be quiet, and be stanch to no inundations.

NUN
Here kneel again, and Venus grant your wishes.

CALIS
O Divine Star of Heaven,
Thou in power above the seven:
Thou sweet kindler of desires,
Till they grow to mutual fires:
Thou, O gentle Queen, that art
Curer of each wounded heart:
Thou the fuel, and the flame;
Thou in Heaven, and here the same:
Thou the wooer, and the woo'd:
Thou the hunger, and the food:
Thou the prayer, and the pray'd;
Thou what is, or shall be said:
Thou still young, and golden tressed,

Make me by thy Answer blessed.

CHILAX
When?

PRIESTESS
Now speak handsomly, and small by all means,
I have told ye what.

[Thunder.

CHILAX
But I'le tell you a new tale,
Now for my Neck-verse; I have heard thy prayers,
And mark me well.

[MUSICK

[VENUS descends.

NUN
The Goddess is displeased much,
The temple shakes and totters; she appears,
Bow, Lady, bow.

VENUS
Purge me the Temple round,
And live by this example henceforth sound.
Virgin, I have seen thy tears,
Heard thy wishes, and thy fears;
Thy holy Incense flew above,
Hark therefore to thy doom in Love;
Had thy heart been soft at first,
Now thou had'st allay'd thy thirst,
Had thy stubborn will but bended,
All thy sorrows here had ended;
Therefore to be just in Love,
A strange Fortune thou must prove,
And, for thou hast been stern and coy,
A dead Love thou shalt enjoy.

CALIS
O gentle goddess!

VENUS
Rise, thy doom is said,
And fear not, I will please thee with the dead.

[**VENUS** ascends.

NUN
Go up into the Temple and there end
Your holy Rites, the Goddess smiles upon ye.

[Exeunt **CALIS** and **NUN**.

[Enter **CHILAX** in his Robe.

CHILAX
I'll no more Oracles, nor Miracles,
Nor no more Church work, I'll be drawn and hang'd first.
Am not I torn a pieces with the thunder?
Death, I can scarce believe I live yet,
It gave me on the buttocks, a cruel, a huge bang,
I had as lieve ha' had 'em scratcht with Dog-whips:
Be quiet henceforth, now ye feel the end on't,
I would advise ye my old friends, the good Gentlewoman
Is strucken dumb, and there her Grace sits mumping
Like an old Ape eating a Brawn; sure the good Goddess
Knew my intent was honest, to save the Princess,
And how we young men are entic'd to wickedness,
By these lewd Women, I had paid for't else too.
I am monstrous holy now, and cruel fearful,
O 'twas a plaguey thump, charg'd with a vengeance.

[Enter **SIPHAX**, walks softly over the stage, and goes in.

Would I were well at home; the best is, 'tis not day:
Who's that? ha? Siphax! I'll be with you anon, Sir;
Ye shall be oracled I warrant ye,
And thunder'd too, as well as I; your Lordship

[Enter **MEMNON, EUMENES, STREMON**, and two carrying Torches.

Must needs enjoy the Princess, yes: ha! Torches?
And Memnon coming this way? he's Dog-mad,
And ten to one appearing thus unto him,
He worries me, I must go by him.

EUMENES
Sir?

MEMNON
Ask me no further questions; what art thou?
How dost thou stare! stand off; nay look upon me,
I do not shake, nor fear thee—

[Draws his Sword.

CHILAX
He will kill me,
This is for Church work.

MEMNON
Why dost thou appear now?
Thou wert fairly slain: I know thee, Diocles,
And know thine envy to mine honour: but—

CHILAX
Stay Memnon,
I am a Spirit, and thou canst not hurt me.

EUMENES
This is the voice of Chilax.

STREMON
What makes him thus?

CHILAX
'Tis true, that I was slain in field, but foully,
By multitudes, not manhood: therefore mark me,
I do appear again to quit mine honour,
And on thee single.

MEMNON
I accept the challenge.
Where?

CHILAX
On the Stygian Banks.

MEMNON
When?

CHILAX
Four days hence.

MEMNON
Go noble Ghost, I will attend.

CHILAX
I thank ye.

STREMON

Ye have sav'd your throat, and handsomly:
Farewel, Sir.

[Exit **CHILAX**.

MEMNON
Sing me the Battles of Pelusium,
In which this Worthy dyed.

EUMENES
This will spoil all, and make him worse
Than e'r he was: sit down, Sir,
And give your self to rest.

[**SONG**
Arm, arm, arm, arm, the Scouts are all come in,
Keep your Ranks close, and now your honours win.
Behold from yonder Hill, the Foe appears,
Bows, Bills, Glaves, Arrows, Shields, and Spears,
Like a dark Wood he comes, or tempest pouring;
O view the Wings of Horse the Meadows scowring,
The vant-guard marches bravely, hark, the Drums—dub, dub.
They meet, they meet, and now the Battel comes:
See how the Arrows fly,
That darken all the Skye;
Hark how the Trumpets sound,
Hark how the Hills rebound.—Tara, tara, tara.
Hark how the Horses charge: in Boys, Boys in—tara, tara.
The Battel totters; now the wounds begin;
O how they cry,
O how they dy!
Room for the valiant Memnon arm'd with thunder,
See how he breaks the Ranks asunder:
They flye, they flye, Eumenes has the Chace,
And brave Polybius makes good his place.
To the Plains, to the Woods,
To the Rocks, to the Floods,
They flie for succour: Follow, follow, follow, Hey, hey.
Hark how the Souldiers hollow
Brave Diocles is dead,
And all his Souldiers fled,
The Battel's won, and lost,
That many a life hath cost.

MEMNON
Now forward to the Temple.

[Exeunt.

[Enter **CHILAX**.

CHILAX
Are ye gone?
How have I 'scap'd this morning! by what miracle!
Sure I am ordain'd for some brave end.

[Enter **CLOE**.

CLOE
How is it?

CHILAX
Come, 'tis as well as can be.

CLOE
But is it possible
This should be true you tell me?

CHILAX
'Tis most certain.

CLOE
Such a gross Ass to love the Princess?

CHILAX
Peace,
Pull your Robe close about ye: you are perfect
In all I taught ye?

CLOE
Sure.

CHILAX
Gods give thee good luck.
'Tis strange my Brains should still be beating Knavery
For all these dangers, but they are needful mischiefs,
And such are Nuts to me; and I must do 'em.
You will remember me—

CLOE
By this kiss, Chilax.

CHILAX
No more of that, I fear another thunder.

CLOE

We are not i'th' Temple, man.

[Enter **SIPHAX**.

CHILAX
Peace, here he comes,
Now to our business handsomly; away now.

[Exit **CHILAX** and **CLOE**.

SIPHAX
'Twas sure the Princess, for he kneel'd unto her,
And she lookt every way: I hope the Oracle
Has made me happy; me I hope she lookt for,

[Enter **CHILAX**, and **CLOE** at the other door.

Fortune, I will so honour thee, Love, so adore thee.
She is here again, looks round about her, again too,
'Tis done, I know 'tis done; 'tis Chilax with her,
And I shall know of him; who's that?

CHILAX
Speak softly,
The Princess from the Oracle.

SIPHAX
She views me,
By Heaven she beckons me.

CHILAX
Come near, she wou'd have ye.

SIPHAX
O royal Lady.

[Kisses her hand.

CHILAX
She wills ye read that, for belike she's bound to silence
For such a time; she is wondrous gracious to ye.

SIPHAX
Heav'n make me thankful.

CHILAX
She would have ye read it.

[He reads.

SIPHAX
Siphax, the will of Heaven hath cast me on thee
To be thy Wife, whose Will must be obey'd:
Use me with honour, I shall love thee dearly,
And make thee understand thy worths hereafter;
Convey me to a secret Ceremony,
That both our hearts and loves may be united,
And use no Language, till before my Brother
We both appear, where I will shew the Oracle,
For till that time I am bound, I must not answer.

SIPHAX
O happy I!

CHILAX
Ye are a made man.

SIPHAX
But Chilax,
Where are her Women?

CHILAX
None but your Graces Sister,
Because she would have it private to the World yet,
Knows of this business.

SIPHAX
I shall thank thee, Chilax,
Thou art a careful man.

CHILAX
Your Graces Servant.

SIPHAX
I'll find a fit place for thee.

CHILAX
If you will not,
There's a good Lady will, she points ye forward,
Away and take your fortune; not a word, Sir:
So, you are greas'd I hope.

[Exit **SIPHAX** and **CLOE**, manet **CHILAX**.

[Enter **STREMON**, **FOOL** and **BOY**.

CHILAX
Stremon, Fool, Picus,
Where have you left your Lord?

STREMON
I' th' Temple, Chilax.

CHILAX
Why are ye from him?

STREMON
Why, the King is with him,
And all the Lords.

CHILAX
Is not the Princess there too?

STREMON
Yes.
And the strangest Coil amongst 'em; She weeps bitterly:
The King entreats, and frowns, my Lord like Autumn
Drops off his hopes by handfulls, all the Temple
Sweats with this Agony.

CHILAX
Where's young Polydor?

STREMON
Dead, as they said, o' th' sudden.

CHILAX
Dead?

STREMON
For certain,
But not yet known abroad.

CHILAX
There's a new trouble,
A brave young man he was; but we must all dye.

STREMON
Did not the General meet you this morning
Like a tall Stallion Nun?

CHILAX
No more o' that, Boy.

STREMON
You had been ferretting.

CHILAX
That's all one, Fool;
My Master Fool that taught my wits to traffick,
What has your Wisedom done? how have you profited?
Out with your Audit: come, you are not empty,
Put out mine eye with twelve-pence? do you shaker?
What think you of this shaking? here's wit, Coxcomb,
Ha Boys? ha my fine Rascals, here's a Ring,

[Pulls out a purse.

How right they go!

FOOL
O let me ring the fore Bell.

CHILAX
And here are thumpers, Chiqueens, golden rogues,
Wit, wit, ye Rascals.

FOOL
I have a Stye here, Chilax.

CHILAX
I have no Gold to cure it, not a penny,
Not one cross, Cavalier; we are dull Souldiers,
Gross heavy-headed fellows; fight for Victuals?

FOOL
Why, ye are the Spirits of the time.

CHILAX
By no means.

FOOL
The valiant firie.

CHILAX
Fie, fie, no.

FOOL
Be-lee me, Sir.

CHILAX
I wou'd I cou'd, Sir.

FOOL
I will satisfie ye.

CHILAX
But I will not content you; alas poor Boy,
Thou shew'st an honest Nature, weepst for thy Master,
There's a red Rogue to buy thee Handkerchiefs.

FOOL
He was an honest Gentleman, I have lost too.

CHILAX
You have indeed your labour, Fool; but Stremon,
Dost thou want money too? no Vertue living?
No firking out at fingers ends?

STREMON
It seems so.

CHILAX
Will ye all serve me?

STREMON
Yes, when ye are Lord General,
For less I will not go.

CHILAX
There's Gold for thee then,
Thou hast a Souldiers mind. Fool—

FOOL
Here, your first man.

CHILAX
I will give thee for thy Wit, for 'tis a fine wit,
A dainty diving Wit, hold up, just nothing,
Go graze i' th' Commons, yet I am merciful—
There's six-pence: buy a Saucer, steal an old Gown,
And beg i' th' Temple for a Prophet, come away Boys,
Let's see how things are carried, Fool, up Sirrah,
You may chance get a dinner: Boy, your preferment
I'll undertake, for your brave Masters sake,
You shall not perish.

FOOL
Chilax.

CHILAX
Please me well, Fool.
And you shall light my pipes: away to the Temple.
But stay, the King's here, sport upon sport, Boys.

[Enter **KING**, **LORDS**, **SIPHAX** kneeling, **CLOE** with a Vail.

KING
What would you have, Captain?
Speak suddenly, for I am wondrous busie.

SIPHAX
A pardon, Royal Sir.

KING
For what?

SIPHAX
For that
Which was Heaven's Will, should not be mine alone, Sir;
My marrying with this Lady.

KING
It needs no pardon,
For Marriage is no Sin.

SIPHAX
Not in it self, Sir;
But in presuming too much: yet Heaven knows,
So does the Oracle that cast it on me,
And—the Princess, royal Sir.

KING
What Princess?

SIPHAX
O be not angry my dread King, your Sister.

KING
My Sister; she's i' th' Temple, Man.

SIPHAX
She is here, Sir.

LORD
The Captain's mad, she's kneeling at the Altar.

KING

I know she is; with all my heart good Captain,
I do forgive ye both: be unvail'd, Lady.

[Puts off her Vail.

Will ye have more forgiveness? the man's frantick,
Come let's go bring her out: God give ye joy, Sir.

SIPHAX
How, Cloe? my old Cloe?

[Exit **KING**, **LORDS**.

CLOE
Even the same, Sir.

CHILAX
Gods give your manhood much content.

STREMON
The Princess
Looks something musty since her coming over.

FOOL
'Twere good you'd brush her over.

SIPHAX
Fools and Fidlers
Make sport at my abuse too?

FOOL
O 'tis the Nature
Of us Fools to make bold with one another,
But you are wise, brave sirs.

CHILAX
Cheer up your Princess,
Believe it Sir, the King will not be angry,
Or say he were; why, 'twas the Oracle.
The Oracle, an't like your Grace, the Oracle.

STREMON
And who, most mighty Siphax?

SIPHAX
With mine own whore.

CLOE

With whom else should ye marry, speak your conscience,
Will ye transgress the law of Arms, that ever
Rewards the Souldier with his own sins?

SIPHAX
Devils.

CLOE
Ye had my maiden-head, my youth, my sweetness,
Is it not justice then?—

SIPHAX
I see it must be,
But by this hand, I'le hang a lock upon thee.

CIOE
You shall not need, my honesty shall doe it.

SIPHAX
If there be wars in all the world—

CLOE
I'le with ye,
For you know I have been a Souldier,
Come, curse on: when I need another Oracle.

CHILAX
Send for me Siphax, I'le fit ye with a Princess,
And so to both your honours.

FOOL
And your graces.

SIPHAX
The Devil grace ye all.

CLOE
God a mercy Chilax.

CHILAX
Shall we laugh half an hour now?

STREMON
No the King comes,
And all the train.

CHILAX
Away then, our Act's ended.

[Exeunt.

[Enter **KING**, **CALIS**, **MEMNON** and **CLEANTHE**, **LORDS**.

KING
You know he do's deserve ye, loves ye dearly,
You know what bloody violence had us'd

[The Hearse ready, **POLYDOR**, **EUMENES** & **CAPTAINS**.

Upon himself, but that his Brother crost it,
You know the same thoughts still inhabit in him
And covet to take birth: Look on him Lady,
The wars have not so far consum'd him yet,
Cold age disabled him, or sickness sunk him
To be abhorr'd: look on his Honour Sister,
That bears no stamp of time, no wrinkles on it,
No sad demolishment, nor death can reach it:
Look with the eyes of Heaven that nightly waken,
To view the wonders of the glorious Maker,
And not the weakness: look with your vertuous eyes,
And then clad royaltie in all his conquests,
His matchless love hung with a thousand merits,
Eternal youth attending, Fame and Fortune,
Time and Oblivion vexing at his vertues,
He shall appear a miracle: look on our dangers,
Look on the publick ruin.

CALIS
O, dear Brother.

KING
Fie, let us not like proud and greedy waters
Gain to give off again: this is our Sea,
And you his Cynthia, govern him, take heed,
His flouds have been as high, and full as any,
And gloriously now is got up to the girdle,
The Kingdomes he hath purchas'd; noble Sister,
Take not your vertue from him, O take heed
We ebbe not now to nothing, take heed Calis.

CALIS
The will of Heaven not mine, which must not alter,
And my eternal doom for ought I know
Is fixt upon me; alas, I must love nothing,
Nothing that loves again must I be blest with:
The gentle Vine climbs up the Oke and clips him,

And when the stroke comes, yet they fall together;
Death, death must I enjoy, and live to love him,
O noble Sir!

MEMNON
Those tears are some reward yet,
Pray let me wed your sorrows.

CALIS
Take 'em Souldier,
They are fruitfull ones, lay but a sigh upon 'em,
And straight they will conceive to infinites;
I told ye what ye would find 'em.

[Enter Funeral, **CAPTAINS** following, and **EUMENES**.

KING
How now, what's this? more drops to th' Ocean?
Whose body's this?

EUMENES
The noble Polydor,
This speaks his death.

MEMNON
My Brother dead?

CALIS
O Goddess!
O cruel, cruel Venus, here's my fortune.

KING
Read Captain.

MEMNON
Read aloud: farewel my follies.

[**EUMENES** reads to the Excellent Princess **CALIS**.

EUMENES
Be wise, as you are beauteous, love with judgement,
And look with clear eyes on my noble Brother,
Value desert and vertue, they are Jewels,
Fit for your worth and wearing: take heed Lady,
The Gods reward ingratitude most grievous;
Remember me no more, or if you must,
Seek me in noble Memnons love, I dwell there:
I durst not live, because I durst not wrong him,

I can no more, make me eternal happy
With looking down upon your loves. Farewel.

MEMNON
And did'st thou die for me?

KING
Excellent vertue!
What will ye now doe?

CALIS
Dwell for ever here Sir.

MEMNON
For me dear Polydor? O worthy young man!
O love, love, love, love above recompence!
Infinite love, infinite honesty!
Good Lady leave, you must have no share here,
Take home your sorrows: here's enough to store me,
Brave glorious griefs! was ever such a Brother?
Turn all the stories over in the world yet,
And search through all the memories of mankind,
And find me such a friend; h'as out done all,
Outstript 'em sheerly, all, all, thou hast Polydor,
To die for me; why, as I hope for happiness,
'Twas one of the rarest thought on things,
The bravest, and carried beyond compass of our actions,
I wonder how he hit it, a young man too,
In all the blossomes of his youth and beautie,
In all the fulness of his veins and wishes
Woo'd by that Paradise, that would catch Heaven;
It starts me extreamly, thou blest Ashes,
Thou faithfull monument, where love and friendship
Shall while the world is, work new miracles.

CALIS
O! let me speak too.

MEMNON
No not yet; thou man,
(For we are but mans shadows,) only man,
I have not words to utter him; speak Lady,
I'le think a while.

CALIS
The Goddess grants me this yet,
I shall enjoy the dead: no tomb shall hold thee
But these two arms, no Trickments but my tears

Over thy Hearse, my sorrows like sad arms
Shall hang for ever: on the tuffest Marble
Mine eyes shall weep thee out an Epitaph,
Love at thy feet shall kneel, his smart bow broken;
Faith at thy head, youth and the Graces mourners;
O sweet young man!

KING
Now I begin to melt too.

MEMNON
Have ye enough yet Lady? room for a gamester.
To my fond Love, and all those idle fancies
A long farewel, thou diedst for me dear Polydor,
To give me peace, thou hast eternal glory,
I stay and talk here; I will kiss thee first,
And now I'le follow thee.

[**POLYDOR** rises.

POLYDOR
Hold, for Heavens sake!

MEMNON
Ha!
Does he live?
Dost thou deceive me?

POLYDOR
Thus far,
Yet for your good, and honour.

KING
Now dear Sister.

CALIS
The Oracle is ended, noble Sir,
Dispose me now as you please.

POLYDOR
You are mine then?

CALIS
With all the joyes that may be.

POLYDOR
Your consent Sir?

KING
Ye have it freely.

POLYDOR
Walk along with me then,
And as you love me, love my will.

CALIS
I will so.

POLYDOR
Here worthy Brother, take this vertuous Princess,
Ye have deserv'd her nobly, she will love ye,
And when my life shall bring ye peace, as she does,
Command it, ye shall have it.

MEMNON
Sir, I thank ye.

KING
I never found such goodness in such years.

MEMNON
Thou shalt not over-doe me, though I die for't,
O how I love thy goodness, my best Brother,
You have given me here a treasure to enrich me,
Would make the worthiest King alive a begger,
What may I give you back again?

POLYDOR
Your love Sir.

MEMNON
And you shall have it, even my dearest love,
My first, my noblest love, take her again, Sir,
She is yours, your honesty has over-run me,
She loves ye, lose her not: excellent Princess,
Injoy thy wish, and now get Generals.

POLYDOR
As ye love heaven, love him, she is only yours, Sir.

MEMNON
As ye love heaven, love him, she is only yours, Sir;
My Lord, the King.

POLYDOR
He will undoe himself Sir,

And must without her perish; who shall fight then?
Who shall protect your Kingdom?

MEMNON
Give me hearing,
And after that, belief, were she my soul
(As I do love her equal) all my victories,
And all the living names I have gain'd by war,
And loving him that good, that vertuous good man,
That only worthy of the name of Brother,
I would resign all freely, 'tis all love
To me, all marriage rites, the joy or issues
To know him fruitfull, that has been so faithfull.

KING
This is the noblest difference; take your choice Sister.

CALIS
I see they are so brave, and noble both,
I know not which to look on.

POLYDOR
Chuse discreetly,
And vertue guide ye, there all the world in one man
Stands at the mark.

MEMNON
There all mans honestie,
The sweetness of all youth—

CALIS
O God's!

MEMNON
My Armour,
By all the God's she's yours; my Arms, I say,
And I beseech your Grace, give me imployment,
That shall be now my Mistress, there my Courtship.

KING
Ye shall have any thing.

MEMNON
Vertuous Lady,
Remember me, your Servant now; Young man,
You cannot over-reach me in your goodness;
O love! how sweet thou look'st now! and how gentle!
I should have slubber'd thee, and stain'd thy beauty;

Your hand, your hand Sir!

KING
Take her, and Heaven bless her.

MEMNON
So.

POLYDOR
'Tis your will Sir, nothing of my merit;
And as your royal gift, I take this blessing.

CALIS
And I from heaven this gentleman: thanks Goddess.

MEMNON
So ye are pleas'd now Lady?

CALIS
Now or never.

MEMNON
My cold stiffe carkass would have frozen ye,
Wars, wars.

KING
Ye shall have wars.

MEMNON
My next brave battel
I dedicate to your bright honour, Sister,
Give me a favour, that the world may know
I am your Souldier.

CALIS
This, and all fair Fortunes.

MEMNON
And he that bears this from me, must strike boldly.

[**CLEANTHE** kneeling.

CALIS
I do forgive thee: be honest; no more wench.

KING
Come now to Revels, this blest day shall prove
The happy crown of noble Faith and Love.

[Exeunt.

Here lyes the doubt now, let our Playes be good,
Our own care sailing equall in this Flood;
Our preparations new, new our Attire,
Yet here we are becalmed still, still i' th' mire,
Here we stick fast; Is there no way to clear
This passage of your judgement, and our fear,
No mitigation of that law? Brave friends,
Consider we are yours, made for your ends,
And every thing preserves it self, each will
If not perverse, and crooked, utter still
The best of that it ventures in: have care
Ev'n for your pleasures sake, of what we are,
And do not ruine all, You may frown still,
But 'tis the nobler way, to check the will.

John Fletcher – A Short Biography

John Fletcher was born in December, 1579 in Rye, Sussex. He was baptised on December 20th.

As can be imagined details of much of his life and career have not survived and, accordingly, only a very brief indication of his life and works can be given.

His father, Richard Fletcher, was a successful and rather ambitious cleric. From being the Dean of Peterborough he moved on to become the Bishop of Bristol, Bishop of Worcester and finally, shortly before his death, the Bishop of London. He was also the chaplain to Queen Elizabeth.

When he was Dean of Peterborough, Richard Fletcher, witnessed the execution of Mary, Queen of Scots. It was said he "knelt down on the scaffold steps and started to pray out loud and at length, in a prolonged and rhetorical style, as though determined to force his way into the pages of history". He cried out at her death, "So perish all the Queen's enemies!" All very dramatic but the family did have strong links to the Arts.

Young Fletcher appears at the very young age of eleven to have entered Corpus Christi College at Cambridge University in 1591. There are no records that he ever took a degree but there is some small evidence that he was being prepared for a career in the church.

However what is clear is that this was soon abandoned as he joined the stream of people who would leave University and decamp to the more bohemian life of commercial theatre in London.

Unfortunately his father fell out with Queen Elizabeth but appears to have been on his way to rehabilitation before his death in 1596. At his death he was, however, mired in debt.

The upbringing of the now teenage Fletcher and his seven siblings now passed to his paternal uncle, the poet and minor official Giles Fletcher. Giles, who had the patronage of the Earl of Essex may have been a liability rather than an advantage to the young Fletcher. With Essex involved in the failed rebellion against Elizabeth Giles was also tainted by association.

By 1606 John Fletcher appears to have equipped himself with the talents to become a playwright. Initially this appears to have been for the Children of the Queen's Revels, then performing at the Blackfriars Theatre.

Commendatory verses by Richard Brome in the Beaumont and Fletcher 1647 folio place Fletcher in the company of Ben Jonson, although it is not known when this friendship began. Jonson, of course, was a leviathan of English Literature, so admired that many of his literary friends and colleagues were simply known as 'Sons of Ben'. Fletcher's frequent early collaborator, Francis Beaumont, was also a friend of Jonson's.

Fletcher's early career was marked by one significant failure; The Faithful Shepherdess, his adaptation of Giovanni Battista Guarini's Il Pastor Fido, which was performed by the Blackfriars Children in 1608. In the preface to the printed edition of his play, Fletcher explained the failure as due to his audience's faulty expectations. They expected a pastoral tragicomedy to feature dances, comedy, and murder, with the shepherds presented in conventional stereotypes – as Fletcher put it, wearing "gray cloaks, with curtailed dogs in strings." Fletcher's preface is however best known for its pithy definition of tragicomedy: "A tragicomedy is not so called in respect of mirth and killing, but in respect it wants [i.e., lacks] deaths, which is enough to make it no tragedy; yet brings some near it, which is enough to make it no comedy." A comedy, he went on to say, must be "a representation of familiar people." His preface is critical of drama that features characters whose action violates nature.

In that case, Fletcher appears to have been developing a new style faster than audiences could comprehend. By 1609, however, he had found his stride. With Beaumont, he wrote Philaster, which became a hit for the King's Men and began a profitable association between Fletcher and that company. Philaster appears also to have begun a trend for tragicomedy. Fletcher's influence has also been said to have inspired some features of Shakespeare's late romances, and certainly his influence on the tragicomic work of other playwrights is even more marked.

By the middle of the 1610s, Fletcher's plays had achieved a popularity that rivalled Shakespeare's and cemented the pre-eminence of the King's Men in Jacobean London. After Beaumont's retirement, necessitated by ill-health, and then his early death in 1616, Fletcher continued working, both singly and in collaboration, until his death in 1625. By that time, he had produced, or had been credited with, close to fifty plays. This body of work remained a major part of the King's Men's repertory until the closing of the theatres in 1642 due to the Civil War.

At the beginning of his career Fletcher's most important collaborator was Francis Beaumont. The two wrote together for close to a decade, first for the Children of the Queen's Revels, and then for the King's Men. According to an anecdote transmitted or invented by John Aubrey, they also lived together in Bankside, sharing clothes and having "one wench in the house between them." This domestic arrangement, if it existed, was ended by Beaumont's marriage in 1613, and their dramatic partnership ended after Beaumont fell ill, probably of a stroke, that same year.

At this point Fletcher had written many plays with Beaumont and several others on his own. He seems to have been regarded as quite a talent although it should be remembered that playwrights were required to be prolific, to easily work with other collaborators and to produce work of quality and commercial appeal very quickly.

The King's Men, run by Philip Henslowe, was the most prestigious of the theatre companies and Fletcher now had an increasingly close association with it.

Fletcher collaborated with Shakespeare on Henry VIII, The Two Noble Kinsmen, and the now lost Cardenio, which some scholars say was the basis for Lewis Theobald's play Double Falsehood. (Theobald is regarded as one of the best Shakespearean editors. Whether his play is based on Cardenio or on some other is not absolutely known although Theobald certainly promoted it as his revision of the lost Shakespeare/Fletcher play.)

A play that Fletcher also wrote by himself at this time, The Woman's Prize or the Tamer Tamed, is also regarded as a sequel to The Taming of the Shrew.

In 1616, with the death of Shakespeare, Fletcher now appears to have entered into an enhanced arrangement with the King's Men on very similar terms to Shakespeare's. Fletcher would now write exclusively for the King's Men until his own death almost a decade later.

As well as continuing his solo productions Fletcher was still collaborating with other playwrights, mainly Philip Massinger, who, in turn, would succeed him as the in-house playwright for the King's Men.

Fletcher's popularity continued throughout his life; indeed during the winter of 1621, he had three of his plays performed at court. His mastery is most notable in two dramatic types; tragicomedy and the comedy of manners.

John Fletcher died in 1625, it is thought of bubonic plague which, at the time, was undergoing further outbreaks.

He seems to have been buried in what is now Southwark Cathedral, although a precise location is not known. There is much made of an anecdote that Fletcher and Massinger (who died in 1640) share the same grave but it is more likely that both are buried within a few yards of each other and that the stone markers in the floor have confused the issue. One is marked 'Edmond Shakespeare 1607' and the other 'John Fletcher 1625' refers to Shakespeare's younger brother and the playwright. The churchyards were, more often than not, completely over-crowded and breeding grounds for disease. Precise record keeping was not a practiced skill.

During the later Commonwealth, many of the playwright's best-known scenes were kept alive as drolls. These were brief performances, usually condensed into one or two scenes and with the addition of music or song to satisfy the taste for plays while the theatres were closed under the Puritans. At the re-opening of the theatres in 1660, the plays in the Fletcher canon, in original form or revised, were by far the most common productions on the English stage. The most frequently revived plays suggest the developing taste for comedies of manners. Among the tragedies, The Maid's Tragedy and, especially,

Rollo Duke of Normandy held the stage. Four tragicomedies (A King and No King, The Humorous Lieutenant, Philaster, and The Island Princess) were popular, perhaps in part for their similarity to and foreshadowing of heroic drama. Four comedies (Rule a Wife And Have a Wife, The Chances, Beggars' Bush, and especially The Scornful Lady) were also stage mainstays.

Despite his popularity, and it appears he was held in higher regard than Shakespeare at this time, his works steadily lost ground to those of Shakespeare and to new productions from other playwrights.

Since then Fletcher has increasingly become a subject only for occasional revivals and for specialists. Fletcher and his collaborators have been the subject of important bibliographic and critical studies, but the plays have been revived only infrequently.

Due to the frequent collaborations between all manner of playwrights, and the revisions carried out in later years, having a settled list of authorship to any given set of plays can be problematic. The works of Fletcher and others of this period most definitely fall into this category. It is as well to take into account that during this period theatres were quite often closed either due to outbreaks of the plague or to the prevailing political and moral climate. Printers, anxious to provide materials that would sell, were not above changing a name or two to enhance sales.

Although Fletcher collaborated most often with Beaumont and Massinger, it is believed that Massinger revised many of the plays some time after their original production. Other collaborators including Nathan Field, William Shakespeare, William Rowley and others also can be seen distinctly in Fletchers' works. Many modern scholars point out that Fletcher had many particular mannerisms but other playwrights would also duplicate these at times so allocating exact contributions of anyone to a play is somewhat of a detective case in many instances. However from the original folio printings or licensing via the Master of the Revels (the statutory licensing authority to approve and censor plays as well a hand in publication and printing of theatrical materials) as well as contemporary notes a fairly precise bibliography of the works can be given with only a few plays lacking substantial authority and provenance.

John Fletcher – A Concise Bibliography

This bibliography gives the most likely date of writing together with when published, revised or licensed by the Master or the Revels (This position within the royal household was originally for royal festivities, ie revels, and later to oversee stage censorship, until this function was transferred to the Lord Chamberlain in 1624).

Solo Plays
The Faithful Shepherdess, pastoral (written 1608–9; printed 1609)
The Tragedy of Valentinian, tragedy (1610–14; 1647)
Monsieur Thomas, comedy (c. 1610–16; 1639)
The Woman's Prize, or The Tamer Tamed, comedy (c. 1611; 1647)
Bonduca, tragedy (1611–14; 1647)
The Chances, comedy (c. 1613–25; 1647)
Wit Without Money, comedy (c. 1614; 1639)
The Mad Lover, tragicomedy (acted 5 January 1617; 1647)

The Loyal Subject, tragicomedy (licensed 16 November 1618; revised 1633; 1647)
The Humorous Lieutenant, tragicomedy (c. 1619; 1647)
Women Pleased, tragicomedy (c. 1619–23; 1647)
The Island Princess, tragicomedy (c. 1620; 1647)
The Wild Goose Chase, comedy (c. 1621; 1652)
The Pilgrim, comedy (c. 1621; 1647)
A Wife for a Month, tragicomedy (licensed 27 May 1624; 1647)
Rule a Wife and Have a Wife, comedy (licensed 19 October 1624; 1640)

Collaborations

With Francis Beaumont
The Woman Hater, comedy (1606; 1607)
Cupid's Revenge, tragedy (c. 1607–12; 1615)
Philaster, or Love Lies a-Bleeding, tragicomedy (c. 1609; 1620)
The Maid's Tragedy, Tragedy (c. 1609; 1619)
A King and No King, tragicomedy (1611; 1619)
The Captain, comedy (c. 1609–12; 1647)
The Scornful Lady, comedy (c. 1613; 1616)
Love's Pilgrimage, tragicomedy (c. 1615–16; 1647)
The Noble Gentleman, comedy (c. 1613; licensed 3 February 1626; 1647)

With Francis Beaumont & Philip Massinger
Thierry & Theodoret, tragedy (c. 1607; 1621)
The Coxcomb, comedy (c. 1608–10; 1647)
Beggars' Bush, comedy (c. 1612–13; revised 1622; 1647)
Love's Cure, comedy (c. 1612–13; revised 1625; 1647)

With Philip Massinger
Sir John van Olden Barnavelt, tragedy (August 1619; MS)
The Little French Lawyer, comedy (c. 1619–23; 1647)
A Very Woman, tragicomedy (c. 1619–22; licensed 6 June 1634; 1655)
The Custom of the Country, comedy (c. 1619–23; 1647)
The Double Marriage, tragedy (c. 1619–23; 1647)
The False One, history (c. 1619–23; 1647)
The Prophetess, tragicomedy (licensed 14 May 1622; 1647)
The Sea Voyage, comedy (licensed 22 June 1622; 1647)
The Spanish Curate, comedy (licensed 24 October 1622; 1647)
The Lovers' Progress or The Wandering Lovers, tragicomedy (licensed 6 December 1623; rev 1634; 1647)
The Elder Brother, comedy (c. 1625; 1637)

With Philip Massinger & Nathan Field
The Honest Man's Fortune, tragicomedy (1613; 1647)
The Queen of Corinth, tragicomedy (c. 1616–18; 1647)
The Knight of Malta, tragicomedy (c. 1619; 1647)

With William Shakespeare

Henry VIII, history (c. 1613; 1623)
The Two Noble Kinsmen, tragicomedy (c. 1613; 1634)
Cardenio, tragicomedy (c. 1613)

Wit at Several Weapons, comedy (c. 1610–20; 1647)

The Maid in the Mill (licensed 29 August 1623; 1647).

Four Plays, or Moral Representations, in One, morality (c. 1608–13; 1647)

Rollo Duke of Normandy, or The Bloody Brother, tragedy (c. 1617; revised 1627–30; 1639)

The Night Walker, or The Little Thief, comedy (c. 1611; 1640)
The Coronation c. 1635

The Nice Valour, or The Passionate Madman, comedy (c. 1615–25; 1647)
The Laws of Candy, tragicomedy (c. 1619–23; 1647)
The Fair Maid of the Inn, comedy (licensed 22 January 1626; 1647)
The Faithful Friends, tragicomedy (registered 29 June 1660; MS.)

The Nice Valour is possibly by Fletcher revised by Thomas Middleton;

The Fair Maid of the Inn is perhaps a play by Massinger, John Ford, and John Webster, either with or without Fletcher's involvement.

The Laws of Candy has been variously attributed to Fletcher and to John Ford.

The Night-Walker was a Fletcher original, with additions by Shirley for a 1639 production.

Even now there is not absolute certainty on several of the plays. The first Beaumont & Fletcher folio of 1647 contained 35 plays and the second folio of 1679 added a further 18. In total 53 plays.

The first folio included The Masque of the Inner Temple and Gray's Inn (1613), and the second The Knight of the Burning Pestle (1607), widely considered Beaumont's solo works, although the latter was in early editions attributed to both writers. Fletcher himself said that Beaumont was attributed so-authorship of many works that belonged solely to Fletcher or to other collaborators.

One play in the canon, Sir John Van Olden Barnavelt, existed in manuscript and was not published till 1883.

www.ingramcontent.com/pod-product-compliance
Lightning Source LLC
Chambersburg PA
CBHW060115050426
42448CB00010B/1873